THIS IS ~~NOT~~ A SAFE SPACE:

Creating Human Connection in a World That Often Fails to Hear

by
Abi Canepa-Anson

Conscious Dreams
PUBLISHING

Published by Conscious Dreams Publishing
www.consciousdreamspublishing.com

Cover Designed by: Abi Canepa-Anson

Edited by: Rhoda Molife, Molah Media Ltd

Formatted by: Oksana Kosovan

ISBN: 978-1-918992-08-3

Dedication

To Adebayo

Contents

Part I

Introduction

Adebayo

On 4 October 2017, I received a call from the coroner's office. My youngest brother, Adebayo, was dead. He was 41.

You can imagine my horror. The news was not only unexpected, it was shocking... devastating. It made no sense and felt at odds with the way things were supposed to happen. I had spoken with him days before. What made it even more perplexing was that it had taken several days before anyone thought to contact me, his next of kin, or our family. He was found dead on the Friday. I was informed on Tuesday.

The cause of death was unclear. I was told he had died of schizoaffective disorder. I remember thinking, *How does someone die of a psychiatric diagnosis?* It would have made more sense to say that he died from the strain of trying to live with a label he repeatedly rejected, and from the effects of medications he insisted were doing him more harm than good.

No one was available for a follow-up, nor were they available to offer me any feedback, acknowledgement or recognition of either his grievances or mine, even after his death. The inquest reached its conclusion and, in effect, that call marked the administrative end of his life. But for me, it marked the beginning of something else entirely.

In the wake of Adebayo's death, I found myself unable to look away from my grief, from psychiatry and psychology as professions, and from what they claim to heal and protect. What had once felt abstract or theoretical, i.e., the authority of diagnosis, the silencing power of institutions, and the effects of structural and institutional racism became painfully concrete. His death forced a reckoning with systems that could name him, medicate him, and close his case, yet could not truly hear him while he was alive.

For a period, Adebayo had lived with me, and we navigated his adolescence together. This was a time of intense physical and psychological change, a developmental stage marked by restlessness, emotional volatility, sensitivity and contradiction, as well as emerging logic and a growing need to make sense of the world. The teen years are a period where we are carefree and armed with wit, yet one we struggle with for its impulsivity and the belief that anything is possible. Despite this push for independence, parental guidance remains especially important.

It is possible that the loss of our mother at the age of 14 was already shaping him, even if the changes were not yet fully visible. When he eventually went to university, marking his transition into adulthood, I took a sabbatical year in Spain. It was during that year that I received a shocking call: Adebayo had been sectioned under the Mental Health Act and hospitalised. Given how well he had appeared to be doing, the news was terrifying and revealed how much of his internal struggle had gone unseen.

Adebayo had become withdrawn and isolated. He was only able to complete a couple of years at university. At the age of 20, rather than being offered psychological support, he was sectioned under Section 2 of the Mental Health Act after complaining of pain on his tongue. He was admitted to hospital, diagnosed with paranoid schizophrenia and immediately medicalised. No meaningful background history was taken. Medical intervention was prioritised over psychological understanding. From that moment on, the diagnosis took centre stage.

Adebayo often spoke of what he called the 'absence of a responsible adult.' By this, he meant someone who genuinely cared; someone who would listen, advocate and think alongside him. Despite his repeated attempts to explain that the medication was not helping, that person never showed up for him. There was no receptive other in place to hear him.

As a family, we had concerns about his wellbeing, but we were excluded from his care because he was no longer a minor. I stayed close to him, speaking with him regularly and seeing him whenever I could. Over time, he was able to describe the side effects of the medication: an inability to focus, involuntary eyerolling, food intolerances, insomnia, hallucinations and severe reflux. These symptoms worsened as the years went on.

He told his doctor and us that the medication was making things worse. The response was always the same: he needed to keep taking it. When he struggled, it was framed as non-compliance. We wanted to trust the medical professionals, but it became painfully clear that they were not listening to him, or to us. They were committed to their interventions and unwilling to deviate from their assumptions.

As a family, we felt helpless. Adebayo clearly needed support but he didn't want to be a burden and felt he could get through to the medical practitioners himself. He trusted that they would and could help, yet he was unable to get the help he was asking for. As he was under the care of the mental health system, we had no say, especially as he was no longer a minor. His care rested solely with the state and the medics who insisted that recovery depended on strict adherence to medication. His experience and his voice were repeatedly overridden by a clinical framework that defined what was considered 'right' for him. It was a frustrating and paralysing time.

Eventually, Adebayo was offered some psychological support. It amounted to a handful of sessions. He spoke fondly of one psychologist he felt a connection with, but the therapy ended abruptly. Other therapists followed, but there was no continuity, no sustained relationship. By then, the side effects of the medication made it increasingly difficult for him to engage at all.

Looking back now, as a psychotherapist myself, I can see how the system failed both him and us, and how damaging that experience was. To see him in the context of his environment and history would have meant recognising the cumulative impact of early loss, adolescence and transition brought on by his mother's death, the developmental vulnerability of that life stage, and the destabilising move into adulthood. Instead, his distress was treated in isolation. Short-term therapy was applied as though it were a neutral intervention, when in fact it is not a one-size-fits-all solution. For someone like Adebayo, the lack of continuity in therapy was not merely unhelpful, it was retraumatising, because each rupture echoed earlier losses, reinforcing the sense that relationships are temporary, care is conditional and attachment will inevitably end. Rather than providing safety, the repeated beginnings and endings destabilised him further, eroding trust and making future engagement feel not only difficult, but pointless.

Adebayo experienced a continual assault on his sense of self. He lived in supported housing where he was dependent yet unseen. He spoke of the wards, of other patients who were severely unwell, of staff who seemed indifferent. He was acutely aware of his surroundings, but the support he needed was consistently absent. This indifference took a toll on his physical and psychological wellbeing.

He began to lose interest in the things he once enjoyed. He stopped seeing friends. His self-esteem plummeted. The energy and enthusiasm that once defined him slowly drained away. The very system designed to help him made recovery feel impossible.

Over time, even basic day-to-day tasks became difficult. Adebayo became a shell of himself. He spoke of support workers who were poorly trained, dismissive and at times openly disrespectful. He felt devalued by the professionals responsible for his care. This sense of being unheard became a constant stress on his wellbeing.

Inevitably, Adebayo's condition deteriorated. And then, on the 4 October 2017, I received that phone call, announcing his death.

He was 41.

Adebayo was a gentleman. He was kind-natured, charismatic and easy to be with. He had a boyish appearance and a warm, handsome face. People instinctively liked him and he was admired for his versatility and quiet confidence. He was witty, sharp and intelligent, generous in spirit and compassionate towards others. His older brother once described him as "remarkably popular, like a politician, winning people over with his wit and avoiding conflict through diplomacy."

At school, Adebayo had excelled almost effortlessly in all subjects. He was also good at writing poetry, singing, sports, and on top of that, played the violin and piano. When Adebayo laughed, it felt as though the world laughed with him. Even in later years, when his laughter became rare, I never forgot his smile. In his 30s, music became his refuge. He collected vinyl, explored different genres and spent hours mixing and compiling music. It was his way of staying connected to himself.

Adebayo was not the same in the years leading up to his death. He seemed resigned to his predicament, and it was painful to witness. Then one day, the music of his life: his rhythm, his presence, everything that made him Adebayo just... stopped. Our family went from living with the sound of him to the silence of his absence. His death was not only a personal loss. It was the consequence of a system that could not, or would not, listen.

When Distress Becomes Diagnosis

In the years following Adebayo's death, I found myself returning repeatedly to the question of how such profound systemic failure could occur, and why it continues to occur for so many others.

At a conference I chaired in 2022 on the medicalisation of distress, the keynote speakers–clinicians and thinkers from different therapeutic traditions–returned repeatedly to the same question: 'When is psychiatric intervention appropriate, and when does it do more harm than good?' Several argued that relational psychotherapy is not a luxury or an optional adjunct, but the necessary foundation of any meaningful mental health care. That conversation felt urgent then because it named something that has only grown more evident in the decade since.

Across the UK, the US, and much of the Western world, emotional and psychological distress has come to be understood almost exclusively through medical terms. Suffering is translated into diagnosis; pain is reframed as pathology. Care is increasingly confined to short-term, standardised interventions designed to manage symptoms rather than explore meaning, history or context. Psychiatric medication and brief therapeutic input have become the default response, not because they are always the most effective, but because they are faster, cheaper and easier to administer within overstretched systems. This shift is inseparable from sustained funding cuts and chronic under-resourcing, which narrow the range of care that can realistically be offered and steadily squeeze out longer-term, relational work.

These developments echo concerns raised decades ago by thinkers associated with the anti-psychiatry movement, who warned that psychiatry risked becoming less a practice of care than a mechanism of social regulation. RD Laing and Thomas Szasz questioned the authority of psychiatric diagnosis to define distress in strictly medical terms, arguing that suffering often becomes intelligible only when understood within a person's relational, social and historical context (Laing, 1967; Szasz, 1961). Michel Foucault further exposed psychiatry's entanglement with institutional power, showing how diagnostic systems can function to classify, contain and discipline those who fall outside social norms (Foucault, 1965). What these critiques shared was not a denial of suffering but a refusal to reduce it to pathology stripped of meaning.

What was once dismissed as radical or naïve critique now appears increasingly prescient. As mental health systems prioritise efficiency, standardisation and risk management, psychiatric intervention is frequently shaped by institutional and economic logic rather than human need. The result is a model of care oriented towards symptom control rather than understanding; one that manages distress without asking what it is responding to, or what it may be trying to say.

Yet people still need to talk.

James Davies, in *Sedated: How Modern Capitalism Created Our Mental Health Crisis* (2021), describes how contemporary Western societies have come to treat suffering itself as intolerable. Distress is framed as something that should be eliminated quickly; to suffer is seen as a personal failure. When pain emerges, the answer offered is consumption in the form of the right drug, the right intervention, the right solution. Within this framework, there is little space for meaning, history, or context, only symptoms to be managed.

This represents a profound departure from the origins of psychological care. Psychoanalysis and other talking therapies emerged from the recognition that healing often begins not with medication, but with conversation – with the experience of being listened to without judgement, haste or pre-determined conclusions. Speaking and listening are among the most basic human acts, yet genuine listening remains rare within institutional mental health care.

The reasons people seek help today reflect this gap. While some conditions may involve hereditary vulnerability, many people present in response to environmental stressors, social pressures and relational difficulties that erode their sense of safety and meaning. UK data consistently show that anxiety and stress are the most common reasons people seek therapy, followed by depression, low self-esteem and relationship difficulties (BACP, 2023). These are not obscure psychiatric disorders, but expressions of lives lived under sustained pressure, often with limited access to respite or support.

Despite this, the dominant response remains medical. Long-term talking therapies are restricted, waiting lists are extensive and medication is frequently offered as the primary intervention. This imbalance reflects not clinical necessity but systemic preference. Medication may be vital for some, but when it becomes the only or default response, something essential is lost. Research consistently demonstrates that the quality of the therapeutic relationship, i.e., trust, attunement and emotional safety, is one of the strongest predictors of positive outcomes across therapeutic modalities (Norcross & Lambert, 2018). Arthur Kleinman similarly argues that mental illness cannot be understood apart from a person's relationships, history, culture and lived experience; without this context, treatment becomes abstract, impersonal and ultimately ineffective (Kleinman, 1988).

The consequences of ignoring context are not evenly distributed. Research consistently shows that Black and Brown people are significantly more likely to be misdiagnosed, over-pathologised and subjected to coercive psychiatric interventions. In England, Black or Black British people are detained under the Mental Health Act at more than three times the rate of white people. This disparity is not explained by higher rates of mental illness but by fear, stigma and racialised assumptions embedded within psychiatric practice. In the year to March 2023, Black people were detained at a rate of 228 per 100,000 compared with 64 per 100,000 for white people (Gov.UK, 2024). These patterns reveal a troubling overlap between mental health care, surveillance and punishment.

This was the context in which Adebayo received his diagnosis. Once labelled, it became almost impossible for clinicians to hear anything else he had to say. His objections to medication, his descriptions of side effects and his understanding of his own distress were filtered through a framework that had already decided what was wrong, and what must be done. Resistance was reframed as lack of insight. Disagreement became further evidence of illness. Listening stopped.

Coercion in psychiatry is often quiet and procedural, justified as care. A patient is told that medication is necessary, that refusal indicates lack of insight and that disagreement confirms illness. Over time, resistance itself becomes pathologised. For Black patients, this process is intensified by a long history of being mistrusted, over-policed and denied full subjectivity. Frantz Fanon wrote powerfully about the violence of being forced to see oneself through a racialised gaze–as a problem to be managed rather than a person to be understood (Fanon,1967). In psychiatry, this gaze can become lethal.

Adebayo did not die of a diagnosis; he died in a system that could not hear him. His death marked the beginning of my own journey. I felt a profound need to give voice to his experience–not only to honour him, but to expose what happens when a system loses the capacity to listen. Healing requires partnership: collaboration between clinician and patient in which authority is shared, curiosity sustained and the client recognised as the expert on their own experience. In therapy, the clinician's task is not to impose meaning, but to help the person make sense of what feels unmanageable.

Now, as a psychotherapist, I am continually humbled by the people I work with, especially when working across difference. Whether it is cultural, racial or social, therapy demands humility. The clinician must be willing to learn, to tolerate uncertainty and to resist rigid forms of knowledge that risk doing harm. Without this openness, care can easily slip into control and into playing God rather than bearing witness.

Adebayo did not need to be fixed: he needed to be heard.

Learning to Listen

This book is not just about listening but also about speaking and what happens when speaking is met not with understanding, but with silence, mistrust or control. It is about whose voices are heard in mental health care, whose are dismissed and what is lost when systems designed to help lose the capacity to listen.

Each person speaks from lived experience. What is said – what can be said – is rooted in history: personal, familial, cultural and social. The listener becomes a witness to that history. To speak is to affirm: 'This happened to me'; 'this is what I believe'; 'this is how I make sense of my life'. To be listened to, and genuinely heard, is to be acknowledged and validated. The simple act of speaking and listening can be transformative.

Speaking and listening are indeed skills, and while they can be taught, they require more than technique. They demand ethical consideration, cultural awareness and self-reflection. People entering the caring professions should come prepared with knowledge of the histories and contexts of those they intend to support, as well as an awareness of their own biases and limitations, so as not to inadvertently cause harm. True listening is therefore both a skill and a responsibility, grounded in respect, humility and care.

I have spent my professional life listening. I have worked in psychiatric hospitals, group settings, training institutions and private practice. I have worked with people experiencing severe distress, with clinicians in leadership roles, with trainees grappling with identity and power and with individuals trying to make sense of their lives. Across these settings, I have learned that listening is not passive. It is an ethical act.

Listening requires openness, curiosity and a willingness to tolerate uncertainty. It involves suspending the urge to categorise, diagnose or fix too quickly. It means allowing the other person to lead, even when their story does not fit familiar frameworks or established theories.

Many contemporary mental health systems prioritise curing symptoms over entering conversation. The goal becomes symptom reduction rather than understanding. Yet distress does not emerge in a vacuum. It is shaped by relationships, environments, histories and identities. When these contexts are not listened for, treatment risks becoming superficial, or even actively harmful.

Research consistently shows that the quality of the therapeutic relationship is one of the strongest predictors of positive outcomes in therapy. Trust, attunement and emotional safety matter more than technique (Norcross & Lambert, 2018; Wampold, 2015). But these qualities cannot exist without listening.

Listening is fundamental to all therapeutic work, but it does not take the same form in every encounter. When therapy takes place across racial, cultural, social or positional differences, the task of listening expands. It requires attention not only to what is spoken, but to what may be difficult to articulate; not only to individual experience, but to the historical and social conditions that shape it. The consulting room is never a neutral space, and for Black and Brown clients in particular, it carries the residue of histories in which their voices have been ignored, mistrusted or disciplined.

In these contexts, listening involves a heightened sensitivity to power, silence and misattunement. It asks the clinician to notice what is minimised, misunderstood or too quickly translated into pathology. Ethical listening across difference is not about treating clients differently, but about listening differently with reflexivity, humility and an awareness of how inequality shapes what can be spoken and what can be heard. When this kind of listening is absent, therapy risks reproducing the very harms it seeks to repair.

Listening also requires humility. The client is the expert on their own experience. People are often far more insightful about their predicaments than they are given credit for. When clinicians listen from an open place, they may discover not pathology, but intelligence, creativity and resilience. Some of the most meaningful therapeutic work I have witnessed did not come from interpretation or intervention, but from presence and from allowing space for something new to emerge between two minds thinking together.

Listening is not a luxury in mental health care: it is the foundation.

Entering Training

Psychotherapy training does not simply teach theory or technique; it teaches a way of seeing the world. It shapes what counts as knowledge, whose experiences are taken seriously and what is rendered invisible. Long before a clinician sits with a client, their perception has already been trained.

I entered psychotherapy training curious, open and willing to change and be changed. I did not believe psychoanalysis held all the answers to human suffering, but I wanted to understand what it could offer. Like analysis itself, training is a process you enter without knowing how it will transform you. You think you know what you are searching for, only to discover questions you had not yet learned how to ask.

Personal therapy, or personal analysis, is a cornerstone of most psychotherapy training programmes. The reasoning is sound: to sit with another person's pain, you must first have sat with your own. To recognise defensiveness, projection or transference in a client, you must have encountered these patterns in yourself. The work is not merely intellectual, it is experiential. You cannot teach someone to listen deeply if they have never been deeply listened to.

My own analysis was both difficult and illuminating. It forced me to confront patterns I had long avoided such as relational dynamics, unprocessed grief and the ways in which I had learned to protect myself at the cost of genuine connection. There were moments of profound discomfort, sessions where I wanted to flee and interpretations that felt too close to the bone. But there were also moments of unexpected clarity, where something previously unconscious became visible, and with that visibility came the possibility of change.

This experience–of being held, challenged and allowed to unfold without judgement–became the template for how I hoped to work with others. I learned that the therapist's primary task is not to solve problems but to create conditions in which the client can begin to see themselves differently. It is not about providing answers but about sustaining curiosity long enough for new questions to emerge. Yet what I did not anticipate during training was how much of what was taught would feel quietly excluding.

Psychoanalytic theory, as it is commonly taught, is rooted in European history and cultural assumptions. Its foundational thinkers, Freud, Klein, Winnicott and Bion, observed, theorised and wrote within a world that centred whiteness as the norm.

This is rarely named explicitly, yet it shapes the canon: who is cited, whose inner lives are explored and which experiences are considered psychologically meaningful.

As a person of colour in training, I often felt a subtle dissonance. The theories were sophisticated and internally coherent, yet they rarely reflected lives like mine or the lives of many of the people I hoped to work with. Very few Black analysts were referenced. Fewer still were treated as foundational thinkers. Race, when mentioned at all, was often positioned as external to the psyche – something social rather than something that actively shapes inner life.

This omission matters.

When training frameworks fail to engage with race, power and history, they implicitly teach that these forces are secondary to psychological development. Distress is located inside the individual, disconnected from the social realities that shape identity, safety and belonging. In this way, whiteness operates not as a topic of study, but as an invisible organising principle.

Caucasian whiteness is not merely a racial identity; it is an ideology that establishes itself as the cultural norm. It is rarely experienced as 'race' by those who inhabit it. Instead, it functions as neutrality or the unmarked standard against which all others are measured. This invisibility allows whiteness to remain unexamined, even as it structures institutions, curricula and clinical assumptions (Ryde, 2009; hooks, 2000).

Dorothy Holmes, a Black psychoanalyst, has written extensively about what she calls the 'colour-blind' stance in psychoanalysis; this is the assumption that if we simply treat everyone the same, race will not matter. But this stance is itself a form of erasure. It denies the reality that race profoundly shapes how a person is seen, heard and responded to, both in the world and in the consulting room (Holmes, 1992, 2016).

Consider, for example, how clinical concepts travel across difference. When Melanie Klein wrote about envy, or when Wilfred Bion theorised about containment, they drew on their own experiences and cultural contexts. These concepts are powerful but they are not universal. To apply them uncritically to clients from different backgrounds risks imposing meanings that do not fit and missing meanings that do.

Farhad Dalal, in his book, *Race, Colour and the Processes of Racialization* (2002), argues that psychoanalysis has historically treated race as an add-on rather than as central to identity formation. He challenges the field to recognise that racialisation, i.e., the process by which people are assigned racial categories and meanings, is not external to psychological life but constitutive of it. From birth, Black and Brown children are subjected to social narratives about who they are, what they are capable of and where they belong. These narratives become internalised, shaping self-concept, relationships and emotional life.

To ignore this is not neutrality. It is blindness.

What Gets Lost

During my training, I encountered brilliant supervisors and thoughtful peers. I was introduced to texts that opened new ways of thinking about unconscious life, relational patterns and the therapeutic process. Psychoanalysis, at its best, offers profound insights into how we defend against pain, how we repeat what we cannot remember and how relationships become sites of both wounding and healing.

Yet I also encountered silences. Silences around colonialism and its psychological legacies. Silences around how racial trauma is transmitted across generations. Silences around the ways Black and Brown people have been pathologised, misdiagnosed and subjected to coercive interventions within psychiatric systems – systems that psychoanalysis has, at times, been complicit in upholding.

Frantz Fanon, a psychiatrist and philosopher who wrote extensively about the psychological effects of colonialism, is rarely included in standard psychoanalytic training. His work, *Black Skin, White Masks* (1952; 1967), is a foundational text for understanding how racialisation shapes subjectivity, yet it is often relegated to optional reading or treated as 'political' rather than clinical. The same is true for other Black thinkers such as James Baldwin, bell hooks and Audre Lorde whose insights into identity, power and relationality are as psychologically sophisticated as anything in the traditional canon.

This exclusion is not accidental. It reflects whose knowledge is valued, whose experiences are taken seriously and whose suffering is deemed worthy of theoretical attention. When Black voices are marginalised in training, the message is clear: these perspectives are supplementary, not essential.

But the point is, they are essential.

To work ethically with Black and Brown clients, therapists must understand not only individual psychology but also the social and historical forces that shape psychological life. They must be able to recognise how systemic racism manifests in the therapeutic relationship and in assumptions about who is credible, who is articulate, who is insightful and who is 'resistant.' They must be prepared to examine their own biases, their own complicity and the ways their training may have reproduced the very structures that harm the people they hope to help.

Yet psychoanalysis has also been a refuge. At its best, it offers a way of thinking deeply about unconscious life, relational patterns and the ways we are shaped by what we inherit and what we endure. It invites humility, self-reflection and an acceptance of uncertainty. Training and personal analysis can strengthen the capacity to tolerate complexity and to sit with what is not yet known.

My training taught me to listen for what is not being said. It taught me to notice patterns – how a client relates to time, to endings, to intimacy, to authority. It taught me to attend to my own emotional responses as potential sources of information about what the client may be communicating unconsciously. These skills have been invaluable.

But I have also had to learn beyond what training provided. I have had to seek out texts by Black psychoanalysts and therapists writing from lived experience of racialisation – Farhad Dalal, Lennox Thomas, Aileen Alleyne, Grier and Cobbs, alongside cultural thinkers like bell hooks whose work has been equally formative. I have had to educate myself about the history of psychiatry's role in pathologising Blackness, from the fabrication of diagnoses like 'drapetomania' (the supposed mental illness that caused enslaved people to flee captivity) to contemporary patterns of over-diagnosis and over-medication. I have had to think carefully about how concepts like resistance, projection and acting out can be weaponised when applied to Black clients without adequate contextual understanding.

This is not work that should fall solely on therapists of colour. White therapists must also take responsibility for their own education. They must read widely, seek supervision from clinicians who understand racialised dynamics and remain vigilant about how their own racial positioning shapes what they see and hear. Resmaa Menakem's *My Grandmother's Hands* (2017) offers a somatic approach to understanding how racial trauma lives in the body. Kenneth Hardy's work on the psychological impact of racialised stress provides crucial frameworks for clinical practice (Hardy & Laszloffy, 2005). Bell hooks' writings on love, care and the politics of domination deepen our understanding of how power operates in intimate relationships, including the therapeutic relationship (hooks, 2000).

Decolonising psychotherapy is not about discarding what is useful. It is about expanding the canon, interrogating assumptions and making space for voices that have been systematically excluded. It is about recognising that no single tradition holds all the answers and that healing practices exist in many forms; some are rooted in Western psychology, others in indigenous knowledge, spiritual practices, community care and embodied wisdom.

My take on it now is that we cannot wait for decolonisation to awaken institutions that have failed to acknowledge what they have ignored. Writing this is, for me, a form of decolonising. But we ought also to take what works. Therapy is not one-size-fits-all; there may be approaches, insights or techniques that resonate, and we can build on what has been learned, adapting it thoughtfully. Psychoanalysis, or any form of therapy, is just the beginning: an awareness, a launching pad from which one can decide what life to live, what to add and what choices to make to create meaning and make life worthwhile.

However, psychoanalysis itself must evolve if it is to remain ethical and relevant. The psyche does not exist outside culture, history or power. To ignore these dimensions is not neutrality; it is erasure. To decolonise psychoanalytic training is not to discard its insights, but to expand them by including voices, histories and ways of knowing that have long been marginalised. What is taught shapes what can be heard. And what cannot be heard cannot be healed.

A Note for Those Seeking Therapy

It is prudent for people to do their research before entering therapy. Much like seeking a second opinion before major dental or medical work, it is reasonable, and often necessary to explore different therapeutic approaches and practitioners. Therapy is not neutral, and the risk of re-traumatisation is real. What helps one person may harm another because people's experiences, needs and boundaries differ; an approach that feels supportive and effective for one individual might feel intrusive, overwhelming or invalidating for another.

Responsibility cannot rest solely with the system. While clients are often required, unfairly but unavoidably, to discern what feels safe, respectful and effective for them, systems and practitioners can help reduce this burden by offering clear information, choice and transparency. In addition, they must actively check that their approaches are aligned with each individual's comfort and needs.

This raises the question so often asked: 'What is the best therapy?' The answer is rarely found in technique alone. Therapy is, at its core, relational. Change does not occur in isolation but within the dynamic between client and therapist, where experience is shaped, reflected and made meaningful in relationship. Through this shared process, unconscious patterns are enacted, noticed, tested and gradually transformed. The therapeutic relationship becomes a living context in which new ways of relating, feeling and thinking can be experienced rather than merely discussed (Stern, 2004; Orange, 2011).

In this sense, the 'best' therapy is not defined by a model or modality, but by whether the relationship allows movement. It is one in which the client feels sufficiently safe to be curious, to take emotional risks, and ultimately, to surprise themselves; this means discovering responses, meanings and possibilities that were previously unavailable. Here are some questions to consider when seeking a therapist:

- Do I feel heard and respected in the initial consultation?
- Does this person make space for my cultural, racial or social identity, or do they seem to dismiss or minimise these aspects of who I am?
- Can I imagine myself being vulnerable with this person?
- Do they acknowledge the limits of their own knowledge and express willingness to learn?

- Do they offer transparency about their approach, their training and what I can expect from the work?
- If something doesn't feel right, do I feel able to name it, and do they respond with openness rather than defensiveness?

This is not an exhaustive list, but the questions point towards the relational foundations that make therapy effective. The method matters less than the quality of attention, the capacity for attunement and the willingness to meet you as a full person – not as a diagnosis, not as a problem to be solved, but as someone whose experience, however painful or confusing, makes sense within the context of your life.

The Ongoing Work

Training does not end when you qualify. The work of becoming a therapist is ongoing, iterative and lifelong. It requires continued supervision, personal therapy, reading, reflection and a willingness to be challenged by clients, peers and the world.

I continue to learn from the people I work with. They teach me about resilience, about the creativity of survival and about the ways people find meaning even in unbearable circumstances. They remind me that my role is not to know but to accompany, to bear witness, to hold uncertainty and to trust that, given the right conditions, people can find their own way forwards.

Therapy, at its best, is a collaborative endeavour. It is not something done 'to' someone, but something created 'with' them. The therapist brings training, experience and a commitment to ethical practice. The client brings lived experience, insight and courage. Together, they create a space where new understandings can emerge.

This is what I wish for everyone who seeks help: to be met with curiosity rather than assumption, to be seen as a whole person rather than a collection of symptoms, and to be heard, truly heard, in a way that honours both the pain they carry and the fullness of who they are.

Adebayo never received this kind of care. But his life, and his death, have shaped my commitment to offering it to others. In learning to listen, I am learning to honour him. And in honouring him, I am learning what it means to be a therapist.

Part II

Clinical Stories

Tasha: Where Diagnosis Replaces Understanding

Whilst in training as a psychotherapist, I took a job as a clinical support worker in a rehabilitation centre, knowing full well that it would be challenging. What I hadn't fully anticipated was how broken the system itself would be. Patients, many diagnosed with borderline personality disorder, bipolar disorder or schizophrenia, were routinely reduced to their diagnoses, their legitimate complaints dismissed as symptoms. Staff, underpaid and overstretched, burned out quickly, retreating behind locked office doors to survive their shifts. Neither patients nor staff felt adequately cared for. The atmosphere was one of mutual fear: 'us' versus 'them.' It troubled me deeply that places designed to heal could so easily make things worse.

It was in this environment that I met Tasha. In my first month at the centre, Tasha was extremely late for our first appointment. When she eventually arrived, unexpectedly, she was surprised when she saw me. I was given a look over, not much being conveyed but clearly assessing my suitability.

"I don't want to be here," Tasha said by way of explaining the lateness.

I was taken aback by how forthright she was. Tasha was a Black British patient who had been admitted and diagnosed with a delusional disorder. She was addicted to both drugs and alcohol. Before her admission into care, she'd lived in the heart of the city. She had previously been housed in a local centre where she still felt a part of the community. This feeling disappeared when she was transferred to our ward. As the only other Black person there, she took an immediate interest in me.

"What do you think could make this place better for you?" I asked her.

This was not a question with a simple answer. But I asked anyway to get her to engage with me. The environment was naturally stressful. Living so closely with patients with challenging issues often caused tensions and anxieties. Given the lack of support and her lived reality as a Black woman, Tasha was naturally keen to leave.

"I just don't belong here," Tasha responded hesitantly.

"You don't belong here?" I repeated her words so that she understood that I had heard her, and to keep things open-ended.

"Yeah. I just don't think this is helping. I'm not crazy or anything. What's the point?"

"I don't think you're crazy. So, what can we do about the situation?"

It often feels to me that people who have felt unheard and unseen are very vigilant and attentive to communications and responses. Their safety and further engagement both depend on it. Tasha's response was guarded but honest, showing vulnerability and a hint of frustration. There was also some disconnection and possibly fear of being misunderstood. It was clear she needed to be heard without judgment; I was interested in what she had to say and showed that I was truly listening and not rushing to fix or dismiss her feelings. This is what I think helped to gain her trust.

Over the following weeks, Tasha and I gradually developed a rapport and she became more comfortable with me. She had previously avoided eye contact, crossed her arms tightly and kept her body turned away, as if shielding herself from the conversation. Her posture was closed and tense. But over time, I noticed subtle changes–her shoulders relaxed and she began to meet my gaze more frequently.

Tasha began asking about my use of hair and skin products and where to source them; hospital issued hygiene products did not always cater to her needs as a Black woman. She identified with me and I engaged with that as best I could, always careful not to spark the envy of the other patients. Tasha needed to feel like she belonged. Outside of her own community, the best way this could be achieved was by having someone available for her.

It was easy for her to identify with me based on the fact that we were both Black women but also based on the belief that I would understand and have her back. From an early age, positive identification (which refers to the psychological process through which a person models themselves on another individual, adopting their traits, values or behaviours as part of their own identity) plays a major part in self-development. The first form of identification we experience is often with our parents or caregivers; after all, that's our first point of relating when we emerge into this world. Therefore, identification is closely intertwined with love and compassion.

Some come to therapy because this process has been disrupted in some way, or was not available, making problematic other respective forms of relating. I was given to understand, Tasha's early life experiences were very disruptive.

Identification in a dyadic relationship, such as between a parent and child, depends on sympathetic mirroring, which means being emotionally attuned to the other's needs. Through this process, one reflects and responds to the feelings and needs of the other.

I realised that Tasha required guidance because she lacked basic self-care skills. She needed support with personal hygiene, washing her clothes and replacing items she had outgrown. This care was essential for Tasha and she needed gentle reminders because she struggled with the ability to care for herself independently. By simply being receptive, this proved to be beneficial for the development of the relationship. It allowed her to see I was not a threat. Receptivity signalled that her feelings and needs mattered, fostering a sense of safety that supported the growth of our relationship.

Traditionally, these types of patients with a history of early trauma are thought not to benefit from long-term psychotherapy. It was thought that they were too emotionally dysregulated, too dependent or too manipulative for long-term insight-oriented therapy. Some clinicians believed that traditional talk therapy might reinforce unhelpful patterns rather than resolve them. They are more often offered short-term intervention in the form of Cognitive Behavioural Therapy (CBT) and Dialectic Behavioural Therapy (DBT). Under-resourced services prioritise brief, manualised interventions that can be measured and delivered within a set timeframe. CBT and DBT are structured, time-limited and often cost-effective, making them a practical choice in overstretched systems. All the different types of therapy can be useful, but not for everyone.

Tasha's mental health problems meant that she could not sit in a room or lie on a couch for a whole 50 minutes. She found the assigned room uncomfortable and claustrophobic. In addition, she could not follow the 'rules'. Instead, we would snatch about ten minutes in the kitchen, then in the corridor, then in her room.

She, however, craved being close to someone and there were moments when she cried on my shoulder. These gestures spoke not just to her immediate distress, but to a deeper need for connection, comfort and safety that had perhaps been absent for much of her life. I offered what she needed. After every session, I kept notes and shared what she had confided with the rest of the staff during our debriefs, with the aim of providing her with more consistent care. I also made Tasha aware of this practice as a way of maintaining clear professional boundaries.

Several months into the work, during one snatched conversation, Tasha spoke about her toddler son, Ross. Ross lived with Tasha's older sister. When Tasha found out that she was pregnant, she had expected to be offered a council house, and with that, she could begin a new, better life for herself. However, her then-boyfriend left without explanation. This threw her off course, and after that, her life became increasingly chaotic. Unable to maintain the responsibilities of daily life–caring for her son or keeping a job–she fell into a deep depression. As her mental health deteriorated, her substance use escalated, becoming a way to manage the day from the moment she woke. Inevitably, the situation worsened and her life gradually descended into chaos. What began as difficulty juggling everyday responsibilities soon gave way to complete disengagement. She lost her job and she struggled to provide the stability her son needed. Her depression worsened; to numb the emotional pain and escape her growing sense of failure, she turned more heavily to substances. What may have started as occasional use became habitual, then compulsive.

"I was expecting supported accommodation," Tasha complained. "This is more like the rehab centre where I was. I don't want this anymore. I want to be able to go out whenever. I want to be surrounded by people."

Rehabilitation centres inevitably limit personal freedoms, and for Tasha, this loss of autonomy was hard to tolerate. The imposed structure and boundaries, however, were protective; being outside the centre exposed her to significant risk. When unsupervised, she tended to act impulsively, leave the centre without permission thus placing herself in situations that were both unsafe and detrimental to her wellbeing. It was clear to me that Tasha needed psychological intervention in the form of longer-term therapy to help with the multiple losses she had experienced. She also needed psychoeducation work to help her to make better choices.

Psychoeducation is a therapeutic approach that is often more directive, informing patients about behaviours that contribute to their ill-health and are no longer serving them. It allows individuals to better understand the connection between their thoughts, emotions and actions. For Tasha and patients facing similar challenges, without this foundational understanding, making lasting change is difficult. DBT also plays a role here as it balances two seemingly opposing ideas: acceptance and change. It validates a person's current experience while simultaneously helping them develop skills to build a life that feels more stable and worth living. However, these approaches are most effective if applied consistently. Working irregular shifts meant that I could not do this. There was only so much one person could do within a system that was under-resourced and overstretched.

In retrospect, I recognise that I may have taken on something of an impossible task–trying to offer the kind of consistent, dedicated care these patients needed within a setting that lacked the structural support to sustain it. This kind of help required long-term commitment, relational continuity and adequate funding, all of which were in short supply. I did receive some supervision during my training, which helped.

"Do you feel truly ready to be fully independent? Independence requires you to be able to look after yourself. Can you demonstrate this? Perhaps you can practice here. We can talk about getting there together." I proposed this to Tasha in one of our sessions.

"Perhaps." Tasha looked at her feet. She was finding the conversation difficult and eventually lost interest.

A few weeks later, I escorted Tasha into town. It wasn't quite the freedom that she was looking for, but it was a start. I hoped she could benefit from the experience, even with an escort, and that it would provide a bridge towards regaining her independence.

"I know people back in the city centre, even my nail salon," Tasha said.

"Does that make you want to return there?" I asked.

"Yeah, of course. I like the city centre. I like the people. But what I really want is to take care of Ross. But it's not going to happen. I'm stuck here." Tasha kicked at a bottle abandoned on the pavement.

"I hope that can happen for you. I'll let the site manager know that's what you want."

Tasha talked more about missing Ross. She wanted to be reunited with him but accepted this would only work for short periods. For some reason, it was all too overwhelming for her and I sensed that she wasn't ready to say why. Eventually, I did find out why. In her mind, Ross was better off in the care of her sister. At the same time, she found it excruciatingly difficult that he no longer remembered her. When Ross cried, he wanted his aunt, not Tasha. She felt sad and anxious that he may not remember her or feel safe with her in the future.

Though she was sad to hear that Ross was better in her sister's care 'for now', it was also heartening to see her taking responsibility by admitting her limitations and acknowledging that the crisis may be temporary. There was hope there, motivated by the love she had for her son. It was essential that Tasha held onto this, and perhaps it could be the goal that would help her turn things around.

Tasha had a close friend, Mia, who she hoped to move in with when she left the facility. However, Tasha was afraid that Mia would reject her because of her history of addiction, which she knew of and had warned Tasha many-a-times about. However, Tasha had limited options as she couldn't live with sister.

"Why can't you live with your sister?"

"I just can't," she said very firmly.

Sensing her irritation, I remained silent.

In the following session, Tasha revealed more. Her sister often worked night shifts as a nurse; while she was at work, her sister's partner at the time, threw drug and alcohol-fuelled parties. At one of these parties, when everyone was intoxicated, he came onto her inappropriately. Tasha found the whole episode confusing and deeply distressing. When she tearfully explained what had happened, her sister didn't believe her.

"I couldn't believe my own sister didn't believe me. She's meant to be there for me. Of course, I was very upset, but mainly just angry." Tasha's shoulders hunched, a tension rising in her body.

I interpreted this posture as an external shell that came up whenever she was afraid. It was the same shell that made the staff afraid of Tasha when ironically, she adopted it because she was afraid of them. It was protective. One thing that Tasha often said was that she was "sick and tired" of being misunderstood and blamed; this was likely her being stereotyped as just another angry Black woman.

After the painful episode, Tasha became distrustful of her sister and no longer felt safe in her home. She then turned to others, particularly men, to validate her. This search for someone to care for her, a paternal figure even, led to the lifestyle that had gone on to consume her life, which included addiction.

Eventually, she dropped out of college. Nobody even seemed to notice, let alone care. Her parents had not attended college, and her friends had similarly dropped out to have children. Those who found out simply shrugged and showed no interest in how this would impact her future. It was becoming clear that she had a poor sense of responsibility when it came to lifestyle choices. The childhood home, being chaotic and unpredictable, probably contributed. Her mother had lots of partners and a series of temporary jobs, and her father was a ghost that showed up now and again. So, there had been no one to teach her how to regulate emotions or set goals. As a teenager, she had skipped school with no consequences. Poor choices weren't accidents but a pattern born out of specific situations.

Through these experiences, Tasha had lived with a feeling that people didn't understand her, whether these were parents, teachers, and now the staff and fellow patients. Where Tasha expected sympathy from those around her, she was met with condemnation. In truth, Tasha confessed that she had finally stopped trying with them. All of this doubled her frustration.

Tasha's feeling of alienation was not limited to the rehabilitation centre. Rather, the centre mirrored the alienation she felt generally within society and her own home. She was alienated from her family, friends and her son. Tasha admitted to being difficult, with a short temper, but there was a deep sadness under it all because she had no way of being heard.

We eventually got to a point where Tasha spoke openly with me. She didn't want to lose our rapport. This sometimes meant that she told conflicting stories to make things more 'palatable'. Tasha had been with multiple partners and was unsure about who the father of her child was. There was one possible candidate, Jamal. She had told him that she was getting her life together. In turn, he had said that he 'might visit' and 'might get involved'. She wanted to be taken seriously. She wanted to be *believed*–as a mother, as someone who could love and protect something more innocent than she had ever been allowed to be.

Eight months in and I had worked out that the more we went on trips outside of the facility, the more Tash and I could connect and the more she would benefit. However, my training was ramping up, and I soon had to cut back my hours at work. One day, at the end of a shift, Tasha caught me on my way out.

"When will you be in next?" she asked.

We did not disclose our timetables to the patients because it often led to anxiety especially if, as in the case of Tasha and I, a rapport had developed between a patient and a member of staff. This anxiety often led to harmful behaviours such as self-harm. That would then have a domino effect: if a patient self-harmed on one day, for a reason valid to them, another would hurt themselves the next day, for probably an unrelated reason. The situation would escalate, with patient after patient doing the same. Sometimes, even patients who had never self-harmed suddenly did. It was very hard to predict who was next. On one occasion, a teenager severely injured herself in the toilets. After that, the staff were required to accompany patients when they had to relieve themselves. However, every precaution we took seemed like firefighting because many patients still found a way to hurt themselves.

Self-harming had become a way of seeking the attention that was so often absent. This 'contagious' behaviour was not the only threat the patients posed to each other. General conflicts between them were quite common. Tasha, for one, had an aggressive streak, as my colleagues had told me, though I hadn't seen it for myself. If she had to wait too long or wasn't attended to quickly enough, she would often kick at the office door. The staff felt threatened as a result and said that they often found her to be unpredictable. Furthermore, she had slapped a member of staff once.

"I was being treated like an idiot," Tasha answered when I asked her about the slapping incident.

She felt the need to defend herself, as she had for most of life and was not afraid to fight. I could have taken this at face value, and believed, like other members of staff that she was simply an aggressive person. Nonetheless, I knew there some justification for her anger.

One day, I heard about a disagreement between Tasha and a patient called Phoebe. Phoebe was the most feared of all the patients, in part because she had been there the longest. She self-harmed the most and had a huge influence on all the other patients. However, she was also known for throwing racial slurs at both staff and other patients.

"What happened yesterday?" I asked Tasha about the disagreement with Phoebe.

"Phoebe accused me of staring at her, so I accused her of staring at me."

Phoebe, in fact kept to herself much of the time. However, when she felt insulted, she was direct, impulsive and at times destructive and violent. Other than what had been reported, it was difficult to know what exactly had transpired.

I knew that Phoebe did not respond well to new patients, and Tasha was still very much considered a newbie. Their differing backgrounds made it clear to me that Tasha's presence would shift the group dynamics and likely heighten tensions. Phoebe was guarded, middle-class and white, with an accent that was crisp and controlled. Tasha, by contrast, was Black British, born and raised in south London, sharp-tongued and expressive. She did not shrink herself to make others comfortable, nor did she have any interest in doing so.

Phoebe regularly lobbed racial slurs at the staff. She knew the staff would and could not retaliate. Tasha was not bound by the same rules, however. And remember, she had always protected herself with a tough exterior.

At our next session, Phoebe came up again. She, along with other patients, had insulted Tasha's hair. Phoebe often made fun of Tasha's frizzy hair, and Tasha responded by being angry and confrontational. Of course, Phoebe was looking for this reaction so that she could call the nurses on Tasha.

Tasha's experience on the ward did not at all consider what it meant to be the only Black woman in that space, or how profoundly isolating that could be. No one named it. No one asked her how it felt. Yet Tasha carried it with her every day – in the lingering looks when she entered a room, in the subtle shifts in the atmosphere and in the way her presence was read before she had spoken. She felt it most sharply when she expressed strong emotion. What might have been recognised as distress or frustration in others was often misread in her as aggression. Her passion, her intensity, her refusal to soften herself were interpreted through a racialised lens that left little room for nuance or care.

Even the most mundane aspects of daily life reinforced this sense of not belonging. There were no suitable hair products for her, and something as intimate and culturally specific as hair care became another reminder that she didn't matter. That made it easy for the likes of Phoebe to make insensitive comments about her – insults framed as jokes – which carried a deeper sting. For Tasha, whose identity and self-expression were closely tied to her appearance, this was not a trivial matter. It spoke to a wider failure of recognition, a message, however unintended, that she did not fit in and that the space was not built with her in mind.

Recovery, as it was offered there, came in one form and one language. It assumed a shared starting point, a uniform kind of brokenness, as though everyone arrived from the same life with the same resources behind them. But Tasha had not grown up with private therapists, therapeutic vocabulary, or environments where boundaries were negotiated gently. Her traumas were rooted elsewhere. They were shaped by race, class and generational struggle. The ward, for all its intentions, was not equipped to untangle that complexity.

It was for these reasons that I began to feel increasingly uneasy about her placement. I wanted to transfer Tasha out of the ward. I wanted to offer her something more focused, more attuned. I wanted us to address the underlying impulses driving her addiction, and to make sense of her deeply fraught relationship with her sister–one that carried its own history of loss, loyalty, and unresolved pain. This was not going to be work that could be done quickly or within a standardised programme. It would require long-term, ongoing therapy: a space where Tasha's full context could be named, held and worked with, rather than quietly erased. This was not the right place for her. There were organisational problems. The centre was not properly equipped and only offered a holding space. If discharged, patients often returned within six months to a year. On return, their experience was the same. The cycle did not end.

After a year at the facility, I reluctantly left the institution. My attempts to provide adequate support for the patients, alongside juggling my training, were too exhausting. I couldn't focus well on either and in some ways, overstretching myself exacerbated many problems.

A few months after leaving, a former colleague told me that Tasha had transferred back to the city centre, which was what she had always wanted. She was happy to return to a place with familiar faces. It also meant more opportunities to see her friends, family and son and be in a space where she could heal and not be 'othered'. She didn't have to code-switch but instead could speak freely. There was no pressure to hold it all together as a Black woman in a world that rarely gave her grace. However, I was not confident that her underlying problems would be addressed any better than they were at the facility.

This early experience at the very beginning of my career opened my eyes to one truth. That truth was that the traditional therapist set-up of a consulting room with the therapist sitting in a chair opposite their patient did not work for everyone. For some, that space can feel safe and containing. For others, it feels clinical, hierarchical, and even alienating. I started to see how a structure that we assume to be therapeutic can, in some cases, reinforce power imbalances, evoke mistrust or trigger associations with authority and surveillance, particularly for clients from marginalised backgrounds or those who have experienced institutional racism.

An organisation benefits much from group activity, adequate supervision and regular training. Rather than just learning to understand the patient's needs, we also need to understand the culture of an organisation, and therefore the unconscious processes that prevent people from giving their best.

Tasha's lack of support was not a departure from her life; it was an extension of her experiences. If we can see that people are not 'ill' in the way society prescribes, and that their illness does not emerge in a vacuum but from their environment and life experiences, we can assess them differently and offer cross-cultural therapeutic input. We can adapt to the needs of the patient, allowing us to reach those far out on the margins, who are often the most vulnerable.

For the time being, this vision of mental health provision is something of a pipe dream. Government cuts have left the most exposed with less access to long-term therapy; sadly they are the ones who need it most.

Tasha's story exemplifies the limits of diagnostic frameworks when they replace attentive understanding. Her hypervigilance, pacing and apparent unpredictability were often read as disruptive or oppositional by staff, yet these behaviours were deeply rooted survival strategies shaped by early trauma. Therapy, or even simple relational engagement, required presence, patience and attunement to subtle signals, rather than reliance on labels or procedures.

Her experiences highlight how systems frequently fail Black women in distress, interpreting fear, intensity, or overwhelm through biased lenses. Tasha's resilience emerged in the fragile accumulations of trust: small moments when she allowed connection, stayed present, and risked being seen. Progress was never linear, and the instability of the environment continually tested her capacity to engage.

Working with Tasha taught me that meaningful therapeutic work cannot be confined to traditional settings or time-limited interventions. The snatched conversations in hallways and kitchens were not failures of structure, they were adaptations to her reality. They honoured where she was and what she could tolerate, rather than forcing her into a framework designed for someone else.

Her story also underscores the profound impact of racial isolation within institutional spaces. As the only Black woman on the ward, Tasha navigated not only her mental health struggles but also the additional burden of being misread, stereotyped and culturally unsupported. The absence of products for her skin or hair, the racial slurs from other patients and the staff's fearful responses to her anger all reinforced her sense of not belonging. These were not incidental details; they were central to her experience and to the failure of the system to truly see her.

Tasha's narrative reveals how institutions often fail those at the margins and how simply continuing to show up – remaining present, attuned and willing to meet someone where they are–can itself be an act of resistance and survival. Through working with her, I was forced to confront the limits of the system, the assumptions held by staff and the quiet but powerful impact of sustained human attention. Real care depends on relationships and an understanding of context. It requires listening and bearing witness, rather than quickly labelling or categorising people. Tasha deserved more than the system could offer, yet in our brief time together, I hope she felt, perhaps for the first time, seen.

Emma: The Weight of Being Seen

When I first saw Emma waiting at reception, there was a composed, careful manner about her; she looked like someone who paid attention to the details. Her hair was done up and the colour of her manicured fingernails matched that of her pedicured toenails. Her dress was well-fitted. It was mid-March–not cold but not particularly warm either–yet she didn't wear a coat, leaving her carefully considered outfit on full display.

In those early days, just after I had completed my training, I wore a sort of uniform which comprised of a loose blouse, trousers or skirt and stud earrings. Our training emphasized that less is more, feeding into the notion of the 'blank slate.' I tried to ensure nothing I wore distracted the client from their narrative, making myself inconsequential–a stance that psychoanalysis continues to maintain. But seeing Emma so smart and formal provoked a feeling of surprise, even of intimidation even though

I hadn't known what to expect. I also knew it was important to hold on to these initial thoughts and feelings.

In psychodynamic work, our own internal responses–those first flickers of emotion or instinct–can be windows into something deeper. Holding onto those early impressions meant giving space to explore my own countertransference, i.e., how I was being stirred. The things that surprise or unsettle us often point to the richest places for reflection.

As I walked towards her, she stood and held out her hand.

"Hello," she said. "My name is Emma Whitsun. Pleased to meet you."

I was immediately struck by Emma's assertion and confidence. I probably would not have offered my hand if she hadn't offered hers. A handshake can be interpreted as a push for familiarity too early on; some people find it intrusive. However, if a client offers me their hand, I take it in return.

I introduced myself, and we headed into my consulting room. I had been looking forward to the meeting ever since her first inquiry about booking a session arrived in my inbox. Emma, in her late 60s, was the first Black woman born in Kenya that I had worked with, and who was older than me. Her age had been specified in her message. When I read that message, I wondered what this older woman would want from me. She had tried to make that clear by asking for help with self-esteem and confidence. I was newly qualified, and though I had worked in the corporate world alongside a fairly diverse workforce,

I still felt uncertain, especially when it came to working with the older generation. Our cultural perspective, age and positioning were things I considered, wondering how they might play out in our work.

Ahead of our first meeting, I spent time reflecting on why Emma had chosen me and what expectations she might bring. While it was obvious she knew I was younger, the issue was compounded by the fact that I have always looked young for my age. This had worked both for and against me. The widely held belief is that older means wiser. While we might know that it isn't always the case, it can be a hard conviction for clients to shake off. In many cultural traditions, elders are seen as custodians of knowledge, family history and communal values. From a young age, individuals are taught to defer to older people without question, equating age with experience and moral rightness. It was possible that she would dismiss me as too young to know anything of use and not engage fully.

Normally, my clients entered my consulting room tentatively, looking at me expectantly, as though asking for permission. There was none of that with Emma. She immediately placed herself in the centre of my sofa and took a swig of water from a plastic beaker she must have picked up at reception.

"Lovely offices you have here," she commented. I calmly nodded and smiled in acknowledgement.

"Speakers' Corner," she resumed as we both settled into our chairs. "Such an impressive area. All these new office buildings. Everybody dashing about. Very smart."

I was glad the place was to Emma's liking. Let me hasten to add that I had nothing to do with the external décor and sometimes worried that clients might find the modern, minimalist space intimidating. However, I was struck by the way she owned her space; in fact, she commanded it; it was her ease with the space, her certainty and the way in which she set her own rhythm. It was in her posture, the cadence of her voice, even the slight pause she allowed before answering questions–as if deciding how much she wanted to share.

There was admiration in what I observed, and respect, but also envy. I felt it clearly, that complicated mix of feelings that arose from watching her command space so naturally. Emma wasn't anything like what I had prepared for, but then I don't really know what I had expected. It would have been easy to collapse into the projection, to let the envy become a barrier, or to defensively dismiss what she was showing me. But my work wasn't to collapse; it was to hold these dynamics consciously, to recognise that two Black women in a room together carry histories that aren't just individual. We bring legacies of suspicion, of scarcity and of having to compete for recognition and resources that have been systematically withheld.

Black women have historically been denied the currency of value, as our intellect is minimised, our authority questioned, or our excellence treated as the exception rather than expectation. When that denial is woven into the fabric of the institutions and systems we move through, it doesn't stay outside the therapy room. It comes in with us. And sometimes, before the work can begin, it must be named. My task was to acknowledge that these dynamics exist and that they're real and present. Then I have to find ways to bring this awareness into the work itself, not as an obstacle, but as material we could work with together.

Emma had highlighted how important it was for her to have a therapist. She wrote that her reason for therapy, in addition to gaining self-esteem, was to stop living with regrets, wondering what she could have done differently and move on with life, transitioning into a new era. With her son having left home and her career on the verge of winding down, she wanted the opportunity to focus on herself. Perhaps she had specifically sought out a younger Black woman who was unburdened by her past to help her achieve her wants.

"I was very impressed by your reception area and café," Emma said, having not stopped talking since sitting down. "Very clean. Immaculate. Modern. The person on the desk was very helpful. I just had to say your name, and they were pulling up your extension, offering me a seat, showing me the facilities. Made me feel at home."

Sometimes, when a client first enters my consulting room, they say they don't know where to begin. In those instances, it's my job to wait for verbal or non-verbal cues. Only with time can I discern an entry point, and later, an appropriate intervention. With Emma, there was a clue to be taken from her mention of 'home.' Behind that word was a sense of recognition and relief–the kind of ease that comes when a space reflects standards, care and attentiveness, all of which contributed to what Emma valued.

Emma didn't have any problem with talking. Quite the opposite. While I was pleased that she was comfortable, she still wasn't being fully open. Her talk seemed like a way to stay afloat in a new and perhaps uncomfortable situation.

"You've told me a bit about yourself in the email. Can you tell me more?" I asked when she fell silent; it felt like an entry point.

It turned out that she was an immigrant who moved from Kenya to the UK with her son in late adulthood. Her ex-partner was also Kenyan. This had been her only relationship, and all she had wanted from it had been a child. For Emma, the desire for a child had been clear and singular for as long as she could remember. She didn't long for romance or partnership in the way others seemed to. Intimacy, with its unpredictability and emotional risk, had always made her uneasy. However, motherhood was different. It offered a kind of purpose and permanence she could understand. A child was someone to care for, to raise and to pour herself into. Emma was proud of her role as a single mother; she had raised a son, Imran, who had gone on to attend a prestigious university and was soon to be married to a Spanish woman. She confessed the work had been hard, but she was happy to have done it. At first, Emma balanced working full-time as a nurse at a doctor's surgery with raising Imran to make ends meet.

She ticked off her list of accomplishments in well-defined bullet points. Her manner had a slight disconnect from emotion. She was articulate, and each point came with a knowing attitude that reflected the wisdom gained from experience and the school of hard knocks. Her positioning seemed to say, 'Motherhood. Done that. What's next?' I sensed that she wanted to tell me the story behind the story: Emma wasn't just anybody. Emma was somebody. Yes, she had faced adversity, she wanted me to know this, but also, what did it matter when she had triumphed over it?

Emma wanted to stay with her achieving self in the present. Though her adversity was in the past, it still played into her present difficulties. I found myself thinking about what she was communicating beyond what she spoke of. She seemed to be presenting an accomplished, and if not happy, then content and satisfied self.

Success for Black women is often framed around professional accomplishment and resilience. Emma had much of both. As Black women do not have the luxury of indulging in their feelings, from a young age many are socialized to suppress vulnerability to protect themselves from a society that frequently marginalises and invalidates their experiences. The stereotype of the 'strong Black woman' or 'superwoman' places unfair expectations on them to be resilient, self-reliant and unwavering, regardless of the personal cost. I wondered whether Emma was tired and had come to therapy simply for a new experience, or whether she was seeking permission to lay down the armour she'd worn for so long.

There was also a concreteness in how she spoke, with a focus on facts, accomplishments and the tangible markers of a life well-managed. When survival has been the primary task, feelings become a bit of a luxury, something to be set aside in favour of what's urgent and necessary. Emotions and feelings haven't been prioritised; they've been sacrificed to the work of getting through. Yet it's precisely that emotional connection–the permission to feel, to be vulnerable, to exist beyond achievement–that Emma and others like her most need.

Returning to the age disparity, I reflected on the dynamic this created. Emma's persistent monologue suggested a tone of the older, wiser woman teaching the young one. There was a desire to impress, but more fundamentally, to be seen and recognised. In a world that devalues Black women's effort or refuses to acknowledge their value, this made sense. For an inexperienced therapist, which I was, encountering this dynamic could easily have provoked a desire to prove one's own worth, retaliate or act out. I could have become overly defensive or tried to justify interpretations or expertise rather than listen openly.

Unconsciously, it felt as though Emma was testing to see how much I could bear before she felt rejected. Staying with strong projections – where a client unconsciously attributes their own feelings or experiences onto the therapist – can be difficult, precisely because it can feel as if something is being done to you. With Emma, it could have been easy to feel devalued and unaccomplished; holding on to my own sense of worth was crucial, as this insecurity was hers.

Emma was relating to me through patterns shaped by her past experiences of being overlooked and dismissed, what we call transference, where feelings originally directed at significant figures from the past get redirected towards the therapist in the present. My own emotional response to her, the sense of being tested, the feeling of inadequacy, was countertransference, my reaction to what she was unconsciously communicating. Understanding this distinction allowed me to recognize that what I was feeling wasn't primarily about me, but rather information about Emma's internal world and the relational patterns she'd developed as protection.

In such moments, I often think back to my children's early years. When they were infants, they'd become upset for reasons like a broken toy or balloon flying away. Instead of experiencing that upset solely by themselves, they needed to share it with someone else. By empathising with their frustration and allowing them to express themselves, I offered comfort and understanding. In that understanding, they found space to feel better. My clients often come to therapy simply seeking their hurt to be recognised. They may re-enact painful experiences, projecting them onto the therapist so that they are seen and comforted. Being seen in this way can, over time, bolster a fragile sense of self.

There is, however, a parallel in how a therapist operates. As much as we'd like to arrive as a theoretical blank slate, life continues outside the consulting room, and client material can trigger reactions. As humans, we affect one another. What is important is the ability and willingness to reflect and recognise when this occurs.

Therapists, even those with considerable experience, can at times feel paralysed, frustrated or angry, and even act out when they become the target of a client's negative projection. This reaction is understandable; when under attack, it can be difficult to maintain empathy as the therapist may feel personally challenged. This could be for several reasons: the therapist may have become a symbolic stand-in for a parental or other significant figure from the client's past, and the client may be unconsciously re-enacting earlier relational dynamics. It may also reflect the therapist's own blind spots or lack of understanding.

For the therapist, remaining in a constant state of listening and thinking simultaneously is vital. The aim is not to remain rigidly in a position or become fearful in response to a client. Nor is it simply to shape clients into well-adjusted citizens within a system they may struggle to integrate. Rather, it is to foster honesty and openness, uncover what is truly troubling the client and break through by honouring the client's anger rather than denying it. This involves tolerating discomfort, both our own and the client's, and resisting the urge to impose a premature sense of resolution or normality. Instead, we remain curious and attuned.

This is particularly crucial in the dynamic between a Black client and a white therapist, where the therapist's discomfort can manifest as an unconscious attempt to minimize hurt. A white therapist may avoid engaging directly with race because they feel culpable, being part of the system that causes harm. This avoidance, though perhaps well-intentioned, replicates the very erasure the client experiences in the wider world. What the client is looking for is not absolution for the therapist, but understanding–and at the very least, evidence that the therapist is working on their own blind spots and is willing to learn from their client. The willingness to sit with racial discomfort, to name it, and to remain open rather than defensive is itself a form of recognition and validation.

Gradually, over time, Emma began to open up. There was a subtle but noticeable shift in her demeanour. In the early sessions, she presented with a curated, polished and upright posture. However, as the work deepened, that veneer softened. She grew quieter, her posture relaxed and folded inward. These small but significant changes suggested an increasing sense of safety in the room–an ability to risk showing parts of herself that didn't fit the image she had worked so hard to maintain.

She talked about her work as a nurse. Although technically a freelancer, she effectively worked for one agency. She complained of often feeling overlooked, castigated more harshly for mistakes and not given leeway. She felt angry as she noticed white employees being treated differently. This was not paranoia or hypersensitivity, but a painful aspect of anti-black racism that is not always acknowledged. Emma, who was deeply committed to her work and took her responsibilities seriously, was nevertheless perceived through a distorted lens of racialised envy. Racism does not always operate through overt hostility or direct denigration, though that was certainly Emma's experience. It also manifests as idealisation.

Black individuals may be admired or praised, yet simultaneously envied for their perceived strength, resilience or success. This form of 'admiration' often conceals deeper fears and insecurities, denying the other full subjectivity. The racialised individual is not encountered as a person, but reduced to a symbol, a projection or a latent threat.

This dynamic resonates in broader political contexts as well. The fear expressed by some Brexit supporters, that foreigners are coming to "take our jobs", ignores the essential contributions migrants have made to the country. In cities like London, the success and vibrancy of the economy depend heavily on the labour, creativity and presence of migrants. In both Emma's workplace and in these larger social dynamics, the problem is the same: a failure to recognize the real lives, value and dignity of others.

As a Black woman, I could identify with these experiences. This kind of racism is meant to feel inescapable and one could argue that is precisely the point. Accordingly, rather than focusing solely on eradicating it, the work we do in the consulting room must also cultivate agency and possibility within it. The goal is to hold space for hope and aspiration amidst social unfairness and institutional injustice.

As our work deepened over the months, I often thought about Emma outside of the consulting room. By the time we were 18 months in, our sessions had evolved into spaces for deep, honest conversation. The progress was gradual; there were no overnight transformations. But soon, stories were told in their entirety, pauses were held without defensiveness and subtle expressions of trust emerged. Even with this growth, I could not fix or erase the experience of being the target of racism, nor the pain it caused. What our work allowed was something different: a space to bear witness, to be seen, and to slowly reclaim a measure of agency in the face of enduring harm.

"You are not overreacting; you're reacting to something real." This validation helped Emma avoid internalizing shame.

Emma had a clear sense of what she wanted from her career. She was eminently qualified, capable and motivated. Yet despite her strengths, she found herself stuck–frustrated and paralysed by the challenges she faced in her current situation.

This sense of paralysis was not confined to work; it echoed a deeper emotional pattern. Emma had experienced a history of destabilising events, particularly in the workplace. At various points, she had been let go – not due to incompetence, but often because of workplace dynamics she could neither influence nor control.

Like many people, she needed to hold down a job to maintain financial stability. Finding herself once again in a position where she felt paralysed was painful not only because of day-to-day slights but also because it forced her to relive past experiences – the belief that she was 'not good enough.' The internal response to this needed to be understood.

Emma's worldview had been shaped by repeated patterns of invalidation and she felt exhausted from constantly fighting them. A kind of despondency had settled in, leading to a sense of 'here we go again.' She felt trapped, a feeling common among Black and Brown clients navigating selfhood while confined by narrow societal boxes. Emma had said in her initial email that she wanted to move forward in life. But what does moving forward look like in an environment that inevitably hinders your progress due to latent, structural and institutional racism?

For one session, she arrived with heavy steps, sat down slowly, folded her arms across her chest and persistently avoided my gaze. Silence stretched between us, weighted and raw.

"I wanted to move out of my place," she began haltingly. "I found a property I liked, but the agent refused to even consider my offer. I tried following up, but no one listened."

Then, with renewed anger she blurted out, "Why does this still happen? Is this acceptable in this day and age?"

The repetitiveness of these problems – the ongoing hate of racism – was striking. I acknowledged the harsh reality. But what is the solution when ignoring it is impossible, and speaking up seems to worsen the problem? For Black British people, there is a difficult, intersectional duality: being both British and Black. Whether born here or migrated, England is home, yet one is endlessly reminded of not belonging. This produces not just alienation but a restless longing for a place that feels truly like home – a longing not simply geographical but tied to recognition and safety.

"You are angry about the unfairness and injustice of it all. This repeats itself, and I see that," I told Emma.

Her response? "Not sure it's ever going to change. It was not resignation but recognition of reality.

In earlier sessions, Emma had indicated that racism at work was minimized or ignored. Phrases like, "You're imagining things" or "People aren't used to being served by a black person" compounded her frustration, making her feel that it was her problem.

"It's brave of you to have spoken up at work," I said. "Do you feel you want to put it aside now?"

She paused, smiled faintly and said, "The ambush."

Black people develop resilience against racism, learning to manage their own pain while simultaneously navigating the defensive reactions that racial conversations can provoke in white individuals – what DiAngelo (2018) terms 'white fragility).

"But why put up with the threat of being ambushed?" I asked.

"I need the money, obviously. Some colleagues are friendly. The branch manager appreciates my work. I get satisfaction from helping others feel better."

"So, there are benefits, albeit not enough?"

"Yes."

Therapy allowed Emma to gain perspective on what she could do about her situation, even if constrained. The insight opened the door to agency. Gradually, Emma began to explore other aspects of her life. She spoke about loneliness and the pressures of childhood, where she had been tasked with caring for her family. Though she enjoyed helping, an unconscious desire for recognition had influenced her choices. Intergenerational trauma, the transmission of historic pain, shaped both her reality and her fantasies, influencing how she responded to racist hostility.

Her relationship with her son Imran was another focus. Protective instincts had caused tension. Emma's success as a mother had inadvertently limited his independence, and she struggled to redefine herself beyond that role. Therapy helped her channel frustration constructively. Eventually, Emma planned to save money, start her own business and invest in her wellbeing. She took up yoga, improved her health and gradually gained confidence. Her relationship with Imran improved as she and he communicated more openly.

This is the work that psychoanalysis can do when it attends to the specific realities of Black clients: not pretending racism doesn't exist, not pathologising anger as dysfunction, but creating space for clients to feel what they feel and still imagine agency. Yet this work requires practitioners willing to examine their own positions within systems of power and privilege. It requires training that doesn't treat cultural difference as an afterthought. I have to say that the training I received did not prepare me for a client like Emma. We worked primarily with white clients and understood both treatment and pathology through a white, Eurocentric lens. Much of my learning emerged instead from embracing my own history and identity. This raises an essential question: how does one work effectively with culturally diverse individuals when little or no emphasis has been placed on understanding difference?

Psychoanalysis continues to operate largely within Eurocentric, patriarchal and heteronormative frameworks, preserving historical models rather than evolving towards an engagement with cultural diversity, intersectionality and systemic inequality. For example, the concept of the 'attuned and present mother' is not universal; in many cultures, caregiving is collective, involving siblings, grandparents, aunts and uncles. Those raised outside European norms often experience psychoanalysis as having little to offer them, and this perception is not misplaced when the frameworks we use fail to reflect their lived experiences.

Yet psychoanalysis does provide an opportunity for repair in the form of an attuned other, the therapist, as a way of making reparations for the past. Being attuned is not just about presence in one's own cultural era, but also openness to other cultural interpretations. Emma needed a therapist who could hold the complexity of her experience without minimizing it; who could validate her anger without trying to resolve it prematurely; and who could sit with the reality that some problems don't have solutions but just strategies for survival and moments of reclaimed dignity.

Interactions between Black and white individuals, especially in therapeutic spaces, are shaped by the legacies of slavery, colonialism, segregation and systemic racism. These histories shape present realities, subtly but powerfully. In a therapeutic relationship between a Black client and a white therapist, these dynamics can emerge as guilt, defensiveness or avoidance, often replicating the marginalisation experienced by the client. Silence, when unexamined, can mirror the exclusion and control clients experience in society. Training institutions must address therapists' own internalised racism, which often goes unacknowledged, leaving them ill-equipped to help clients.

My approach was to stay with the pain and uncertainty, creating space where client and therapist could feel safe, understood and engaged in meaningful work. The process required time, patience and consistent presence – qualities vividly illustrated in the series, *In Treatment*, which emphasises the nuanced, gradual work of therapy. The TV drama follows a psychotherapist through his sessions with individual clients, depicting week by week the slow, nonlinear, and often uncomfortable work of building a therapeutic relationship. The series gives attention to the relational dynamics between therapist and patient, including rupture, silence, transference and the therapist's own countertransference.

Emma's growth exemplifies the value of relational psychoanalytic therapy: a collaborative space where vulnerability is met with attunement, authenticity and curiosity. Silence, when filled with presence, becomes holding rather than erasing. Minoritised therapists may offer a particular resonance, but the principles of openness, accountability and cultural sensitivity apply to all practitioners.

Healing from racism is multifaceted, involving mind, body, community and identity. Psychoanalysis must adapt beyond Eurocentric norms to reflect diverse lived experiences. Practitioners must acknowledge that racial difference is a collective concern. Minoritised clients seek one simple thing: the dignity, subjectivity and humanity afforded to any other person, without the added burden of justifying their existence.

Therapy can create the perspective, space and recognition necessary for individuals to see beyond systemic constraints. Even small acts of respect, curiosity and genuine interest can profoundly affirm a client's worth and agency.

Emma's story underscores the ways in which Black women's achievements and resilience can coexist with invisibility, exhaustion and unacknowledged suffering. Her professional and well-presented demeanour, articulate presentation and apparent confidence were all intertwined with strategies for survival in spaces that consistently failed to see her value. Therapy with Emma required more than theory or technique; it required presence, empathy and the willingness to bear witness. Her frustrations with work, motherhood and intergenerational pressures were not solely personal burdens, they were entwined with structural inequities and cultural expectations. Progress was incremental and non-linear: small acts of agency, self-recognition and risk-taking became evidence of growth.

Emma's story highlights that authentic care is relational, context-sensitive and responsive. It requires acknowledging systemic injustices, validating lived experience, and creating a space where clients can imagine a life beyond the roles imposed upon them. Her courage in showing up, speaking truth and exploring possibility is itself a form of resistance and survival. Emma's presence challenged assumptions, revealed the limitations of rigid frameworks and demonstrated the transformative power of sustained human attention and recognition.

Amelia: Birth, Care and the Labour of Visibility

At first, what struck me about Amelia was the hint of self-neglect in her appearance. She was attractive but seemed older than her years. She wore no makeup and had come in her work clothes, marked and stained with her ID badge dangling from a lanyard.

Amelia sauntered across the room, each step slow and deliberate, her gait almost lethargic. Her posture, with shoulders loose was relaxed to the point of indifference. When she reached the sofa, she sank into it, taking up as much space as possible, her belongings scattered across the remaining space. Her legs were crossed lazily. She did not maintain eye contact and seemed distracted by her surroundings, her fingers fidgeting absently with her sleeve. After a while, she met my gaze.

"Sorry, am I too early?" Amelia asked with a pleasant smile. "I hope I'm not intruding."

"It's quite alright; you're not intruding," I replied reassuringly. I am always mindful of the challenge in beginning therapy for most people; it is like venturing into the unknown, and some awkwardness is to be expected.

Amelia had been referred to me through the Employee Assistance Programme (EAP). She worked for a government-funded organisation, and after a telephone assessment, the EAP had recommended six therapy sessions. Early in my career, I had worked with EAP clients and found such time-limited therapy challenging. Six sessions are rarely enough to fully explore a client's feelings. While these interventions can temporarily soothe a fragile ego, they rarely address the root of the problem or support sustained emotional growth. At best, they highlight areas needing further exploration. Some would argue that any intervention is better than none. In my experience, however, well-intentioned but shallow interventions can sometimes do more harm than good. I was always reluctant to take on a case that could not be seen through to the end, but in some cases, I did.

From my initial assessment, it was clear that Amelia would require substantial work over an extended period. For her therapy to be meaningful, it needed to remain open-ended for at least a year. Fortunately, her company agreed to this with minimal resistance. We therefore started working together in early 2019 and in the end, Amelia completed 18 months of weekly therapy, which turned out to be time that proved essential for the depth of work Amelia needed to do.

Speaking to Amelia in that first session, I smiled. "I've read your assessment report, but can you tell me in your own words what brought you here?"

"Work is hard now," Amelia said in a strained voice. "I'm under a lot of pressure. I don't think I'm coping well. But work isn't the only problem. I'm feeling overwhelmed. Alan, my partner, told me to take it easy, to take a break, but I can't take a break. I need the money. When people tell me to slow down, I just feel annoyed. They don't understand."

Amelia had a lot to say. I could hear how overwhelmed, stressed, trapped and powerless she felt. She held herself responsible because others relied on her. Yet there was something more – a sense of just trying to stay afloat.

"You're articulating the problems well, but I sense you don't feel understood or supported, and you can't find a way out," I said.

"I work for fire and rescue services," she continued. "Being part of the team, you can't stop. You can't phone in sick. If there's an emergency, you must respond. All of us are in the same boat. We work long hours and don't always get a break."

"It sounds like there's no room for anything less than total commitment. But I wonder what that costs you."

"I feel like things must change. I can't keep going like this. It's overwhelming. But... I can't change the system. That's only part of it. I feel anxious most of the time."

"A lot is going on," I commented thoughtfully.

Amelia paused briefly, then sighed. "I really feel I need this space to process everything."

"And you have time. You know you have my support now for a year," I reassured her.

Eventually, Amelia shared that she had miscarried at 17 weeks, a detail included in her assessment report. Her account in session was far more detailed. At first, she had kept the painful details minimal, avoiding reliving the experience. This miscarriage had happened about three months before she started therapy, and the grief was still raw.

She described the moment she noticed bleeding in the bathroom. Fear quickly took hold. Alan, her partner, provided comfort, stepping in to manage the situation, taking time off work, staying close, reassuring and loving her. In that moment, his support was exactly what she needed, present when it mattered most.

I could see the same emotions return to her eyes. "You had a painful and difficult loss. That sounds like a lot to go through. I'm sorry to hear this."

After a short pause, she continued. "Yes, it was hard. I feel tearful most of the time now. Little things set me off, but I try to hold it in."

"It's completely understandable that you feel tearful. You're not just grieving what happened, but also the hopes and dreams you had for your baby. Grieving in this way takes time."

"I don't think about it often. I throw myself into work. I'm just tearful a lot. We lose babies sometimes in my work, and when things go wrong, you can't help but feel the pain and loss. Even when things go perfectly, there's still so much emotion and pressure."

It was clear how the trauma was playing out. Work had become a coping mechanism – something that gave her structure and purpose amid emotional chaos. In agreeing to extend therapy, her team had recognised the gravity of her experience and the internal conflict: processing her loss while focusing on professional responsibilities.

I knew that emergency service work must have been an incredibly difficult environment, even outside Amelia's grief. Dissociation would be required to cope with the constant exposure to trauma and the harsh reality of lives lost and crises unfolding daily. Layered on top of that was the complexity of being a woman in a society that holds narrow ideas about what a fulfilling life should look like. Women who do not want children are often pathologised; those who do want children but cannot conceive carry unspoken shame. Our culture largely places family life at the centre of the 'healthy norm,' making it hard to think outside these parameters.

In Amelia's family, having a child was expected. She had been taught that being childless would be a source of shame. Many families fail to question the pressures placed on women. They rarely consider biological, economic or mental health constraints. They seldom see the strength in women who choose not to have children or understand the pain of those who try and fail.

These pressures are compounded for Black women, who face stark racial disparities in maternal health. In the UK, Black women are 3.7 times more likely to die during pregnancy or in the first year after childbirth than white women (Felker & Knight, 2024). Black babies face a 124% higher risk of stillbirth and a 43% higher risk of neonatal mortality compared with white babies (Draper et al., 2022). Institutional racism, socioeconomic barriers and historical inequities affect access to care, often making pregnancy, fertility and maternal wellbeing considerably more difficult to navigate for Black women than for their white counterparts (House of Commons Women and Equalities Committee, 2023).

Psychotherapist Helen P. George's edited collection *Black Women, Trauma and Therapy* highlights how these intersecting pressures of societal expectations, systemic neglect and cultural silencing shape Black women's experiences of infertility and reproductive loss (June 2025). As George and contributors note, the psychological burden of childlessness is both personal and political; intergenerational trauma, coupled with cultural norms that demand self-sacrifice and prioritising others, intensifies the stress and grief of reproductive challenges. Understanding these intersectional realities is essential in therapy, as failing to acknowledge them risks minimising or misunderstanding the lived experience of women like Amelia, whose reproductive choices and grief are deeply embedded in both family and societal contexts.

Black women are often conditioned to prioritise the needs of others over their own. Learning to pause and consider whether pressures are theirs to bear, or whether they can be delegated, is a crucial skill. Amelia needed to discern whether her desire for a child came from herself or from societal expectations. This would take time.

As a psychotherapist, my role is to facilitate clients arriving at their own needs and wants. I will offer psychoeducation when a client is in a state of panic or about to make a significant decision, as was the case with Amelia. The aim is to normalise her experience, reduce fear and isolation and create space for reflection without judgment. Amelia was receptive. She saw therapy as an opportunity to change her life.

"Though it's daunting," Amelia continued, "things need to change, and this is the first step."

"When you say things need to change, what comes to mind first?"

"Well...," she paused, considering. "I get so stressed and overwhelmed. I can't help taking it out on Alan. We're always arguing about trivial things. Maybe I'd like to feel less angry. Just more relaxed."

Her two main stressors were work and her relationship. Unresolved conflict in one area often spills over into another, and in Amelia's case, emotional strain in her relationship intensified stress at work.

"Has it always been like this?" I asked.

"No," she answered.

Amelia had known Alan since childhood; both were born and raised in Zanzibar. Life had taken them in different directions after school, but years later, they met again by chance at a mutual friend's party, reconnected and fell in love. They had now built a life together in the UK. They weren't married but had been together for five years and were deeply committed to each other.

"It felt like destiny," Amelia said.

"You were happy to find each other again," I noted.

They had been happy in their relationship. Alan provided stability; he worked as a plumber around Greater London. They had been trying for two years to have a child. Amelia worried that infertility might jeopardise their relationship. The miscarriage at 17 weeks had been one of several losses – she had experienced two earlier miscarriages in the first trimester, but this one, happening so much later, had been particularly devastating.

To distract herself, she threw herself into work, taking extra shifts and responsibilities. What initially appeared as resilience and industriousness became another source of stress. This vicious cycle of unprocessed grief and trauma, especially in a high-stress environment like emergency services, left little room for reflection. For Amelia, coping and over-functioning blurred. Symptoms such as irritability, anxiety, chronic pain and burnout were possible if recovery time was insufficient.

"I couldn't stop thinking about the pregnancy," Amelia said. "I expected things to go badly. How do women manage? Can you just take nine months off, stress-free? I didn't know how to stop worrying."

"You tried to care for yourself the best way you knew," I said. "Work became both a refuge and a burden, ending up in a vicious cycle."

Amelia blamed herself and, to a lesser degree, Alan. Although medical tests confirmed fertility for both, she shouldered the responsibility alone. It is common for couples to internalise blame after miscarriage, often leaving women to bear the psychological weight.

"Have you spoken about your feelings with Alan?" I asked.

"No, he's not an emotional person," she stifled a laugh. "He's a man of action, not words. He says we should just keep trying. Where do you go from there?"

Amelia felt isolated in her relationship. She could not confide in her parents; she had spent much of her childhood seeking her mother's affection, often to no avail. Her mother's emotional unavailability, compounded by her father's preoccupation with work, left her with persistent feelings of being unseen and overlooked. Amelia had longed for love and support but learned early to look after others, hoping it would be reciprocated.

The first few months of therapy focused on creating a space where Amelia could begin to articulate her grief without immediately deflecting to work or practical concerns. She would often arrive exhausted, having worked a night shift, yet insisting she was 'fine' and ready to talk. Gradually, she noticed how much energy she spent maintaining this façade of coping.

Around four months into our work, Amelia shared more about her childhood. She described a household where emotions were rarely discussed and where her mother's love felt conditional on achievement and compliance. Her father, though present physically, was emotionally distant, absorbed in his work. Amelia had learned that the way to earn approval was to be useful, to not make demands and to solve problems rather than express needs. This pattern had carried into her adult life. With Alan, she found herself cooking elaborate meals, keeping the house immaculate, taking on extra shifts to contribute financially, all while her own emotional needs went unspoken. She feared that if she expressed vulnerability, asked for support or admitted she was struggling, Alan might see her as a burden.

"What do you imagine would happen if you told him how you really feel?" I asked during one session.

Amelia was quiet for a long moment. "I think he might leave," she said finally, her voice barely above a whisper. "Or he might think I'm weak. That I can't handle things."

"So, you protect yourself by not letting him see the parts of you that feel vulnerable?"

She nodded. "If I don't show it, maybe it's not real. Maybe I can just keep going."

But she couldn't keep going, not indefinitely. Around six months into therapy, Amelia experienced a physical collapse at work – nothing serious medically, but her body had essentially forced her to stop. She took a week off, something she rarely allowed herself, and during that time, something shifted.

"I realised I can't do this anymore," she told me when she returned to therapy. "Not like this. Something has to change."

We began exploring what 'change' might look like. For Amelia, it meant starting to distinguish between what she wanted and what she felt was expected of her. Did she want a child because it was her deep desire, or because she believed it was the only way to feel complete, to earn her mother's approval or to secure Alan's commitment?

These were painful questions, and the answers didn't come immediately. Over the following months, Amelia noticed how much of her life was organised around avoiding disappointment, both her own and others'. She worked extra shifts not just for money, but to avoid being home, where the absence of a child felt more pronounced. She kept busy to avoid thinking about whether her relationship with Alan was truly meeting her needs.

Around ten months into therapy, Amelia made a significant decision. She asked Alan to come to couples therapy with her. To her surprise, he agreed without hesitation. What Amelia had interpreted as emotional unavailability was, in part, Alan's own grief and uncertainty about how to support her. He had been afraid of saying the wrong thing, of making things worse, so he had retreated into practicality and action. The couples therapy, which I did not conduct but supported Amelia through, became a turning point for them. They started to talk about their losses together, rather than carrying them separately. Alan admitted he had been scared too, that he didn't know how to help. Amelia realised she had been protecting him from her grief, assuming he couldn't handle it, when in fact he had been waiting for permission to share his own.

During this time, Amelia also began exploring the option of freezing her eggs. This decision wasn't about giving up on having a child but about reclaiming a sense of agency. For so long, she had felt at the mercy of her body, of timing and of circumstance. Egg freezing offered her a way to pause, to take the pressure off, to make space for healing without feeling like time was running out.

"It feels like I'm giving myself permission to breathe," she said. "To not have everything figured out right now."

This was perhaps the most significant shift in our work together. Amelia was beginning to see that she didn't have to have all the answers, that uncertainty wasn't failure, and that taking time for herself wasn't selfish.

By the time we reached the end of our 18 months together, Amelia was in a different place; not because all her problems were solved, but because she had developed a different relationship with herself. She was no longer running from her grief and no longer over-functioning to avoid feeling. She had begun to recognise her own needs and to believe they were worthy of attention.

In one of our final sessions, Amelia reflected on how far she had come.

"I used to think that if I just worked hard enough, if I just did everything right, things would fall into place," she said. "But I've learned that's not how life works. Sometimes things don't go the way you planned, and that's not a failure. It's just life."

We ended therapy with Amelia feeling more grounded, more connected to Alan and more compassionate towards herself. She was still debating the question of parenthood, but she was doing so from a place of choice rather than obligation, and from a place of self-awareness rather than self-abandonment.

Working with Amelia revealed how deeply reproductive loss and cultural expectations can intersect with unprocessed grief and relational patterns. She arrived in therapy exhausted, over-functioning at work to avoid confronting the pain of miscarriage and the fear that she might never become a mother. Our early work focused simply on creating space to slow down. Amelia had learned in emergency services to compartmentalise and push through, but this survival skill had become a barrier to healing. She couldn't process loss because she was constantly moving, and she couldn't rest because stopping meant feeling.

What struck me most was how Amelia's desire for a child had become entangled with questions of worth and belonging. She carried her mother's emotional unavailability, her family's expectations and the weight of cultural pressures that equate womanhood with motherhood. For Black women, these pressures are compounded by systemic healthcare inequities – the knowledge that Black women in the UK are four times more likely to die in pregnancy creates another layer of fear and grief.

A turning point came when Amelia's body forced her to stop. This crisis opened a door to deeper questions: Did she want a child for herself, or because she believed it was the only way to be loved, valued or made complete? Untangling these threads required patience and a willingness to sit with uncertainty. The decision to pursue couples therapy and later to freeze her eggs represented a shift from desperation to agency. Amelia was learning that she could make choices that honoured both her desires and her limitations, that pausing wasn't giving up, and that her worth wasn't contingent on meeting the expectations of others.

By the end of our work, Amelia hadn't 'solved' the question of motherhood, but she had developed a different relationship with herself. It was one marked by self-compassion rather than self-abandonment, and by reflection rather than reaction. She learned that asking for help wasn't weakness and that her needs mattered. This capacity to pause, feel and choose, rather than simply react and perform, is perhaps the most important outcome of our work together.

This case reminded me that meaningful therapeutic change requires time, consistency and a willingness to address not just individual psychology but the systemic and cultural forces that shape our clients' lives. It also reinforced the importance of advocating for extended therapy when brief interventions are insufficient – some grief cannot be rushed.

Jackie: Desire, Shame and Self-Assertion

"I've come because I need help finding my biological parents," Jackie stated.

Jackie came to therapy with a clear purpose. She seemed to know exactly what she wanted to achieve, and on the surface, this clarity can be a strength; it demonstrates intent and motivation. However, a fixed goal can sometimes mask a deeper avoidance of vulnerability.

By focusing on a concrete outcome, a client may unconsciously maintain control over the therapeutic process, protecting themselves from exploring painful or uncomfortable emotions. In Jackie's case, her certainty about the goal might have allowed her to limit emotional risk, avoid confronting underlying anxieties or past experiences, and preserve a sense of identity that felt safe. While having a goal provides structure, it can also serve as a subtle defence, keeping therapy contained and predictable, rather than fully open to the unpredictable, relational and often challenging work that therapy demands.

Despite my concerns, I decided to take her on. I reminded myself to tread carefully; it was just a feeling, nothing I could yet name. Jackie had a captivating smile, often appearing bright and charismatic, but there was something about her that seemed guarded. While I would ask open questions, she would attempt to streamline the conversation and only answer precisely what was put to her. In moments when the conversation edged too close to something raw, she would cross her arms or pull her knees slightly inward, as if protecting something fragile. Still, it was early days, so I took what Jackie offered and worked with it.

It was hard work getting to know Jackie. As usual, I tried to create a collaborative environment. I have often said; you get out what you put in. However, people are different. They are not always responsive in the same way. I can't get a word in with some clients, while others, like Jackie, hardly say anything. In either case, something is being re-enacted. My job is to pay attention to what they are saying and how I am feeling about what they are saying. I could push, of course, but I needed to respect Jackie's defence mechanism; a 'no entry' signal is there for a reason.

Jackie needed to be in control. She was always on broadcast. We were not conversing and it certainly wasn't a two-way street; I didn't feel my input was necessary. This protective display was a way of not being intruded upon. She was an observer and she watched me closely and kept me where she needed me. By only showing a superficial picture, we were prevented from any deeper reflection.

The therapist being used in this way is often a difficult experience. I found myself 'unenthusiastic' about our sessions, sensing that something in the dynamic wasn't quite working for either of us. It began to feel as though Jackie was coming more out of obligation than genuine engagement, focused on completing the task rather than participating in a shared process. I knew I needed to find a way to shift the dynamic, to create a space that felt safer and more collaborative for both of us.

Donald Winnicott, a psychoanalytic theoretician whose work I often return to, introduced the concept of 'play' as central to psychological development. By play, Winnicott refers not to toys or games, but to the capacity to express thoughts and feelings, freely speaking what is on the mind without excessive filtering. It is a form of psychological freedom, a space where spontaneity, curiosity, and creativity can emerge.

Young children naturally engage in this kind of play. Yet many adults struggle to, and often for good reason. When environments subtly or overtly discourage emotional expression, e.g., when a child is told to "be quiet," shamed for crying or learns that certain thoughts and feelings are unwelcome, psychological safety is compromised. The child may adapt by relying on concrete, logical thinking as a protective mechanism, suppressing emotional spontaneity. Over time, this can hinder emotional exploration and creativity, making it more difficult to engage fully in reflective or therapeutic work.

In therapy, creating a playful space allows clients to experiment with thoughts and feelings in safety, reactivating the natural curiosity and expressive freedom that might have been constrained in childhood. Winnicott's ideas help me think about how to support clients like Jackie, whose early experiences of emotional containment and family pressures shaped their capacity for self-expression, reflection and agency.

If curiosity is encouraged by a present caregiver, children can develop an interest in their environment. Unfortunately, not every caregiver has the availability to be both physically and psychologically present. It is worth remembering that in some cultures, it could be the availability of the wider community, and the way in which children are viewed. It is not uncommon to come across cultures where children are expected to be seen and not heard. I've also been reflecting on how, in many Black and Brown cultures (though not limited to these), our emotional worlds haven't always been given space, let alone prioritised.

The idea that feelings are something to suppress, manage privately or simply move past is deeply woven into many of our upbringings. Those with an attuned other get a chance to have their personality nurtured. However, as adults, we lose this innate ability as we become more embroiled in life and its challenges. Recreating this lost space where one can freely associate and explore without judgement is partly the process of therapy. The aim is to get the client comfortable enough to say what is on their mind. To move towards healing, the client must reach a place where they can gradually loosen these defences. In effect, by creating a space that allows for this kind of psychological freedom, they may reacquire, or acquire for the first time, the ability to dream and, in the process, the ability to surprise themselves. It is in these moments, when something unfiltered breaks through, that genuine transformation can occur.

In Jackie's case, this ability had somehow been arrested in development. She struggled to symbolise deeper meanings. From the controlled initial encounter, I thought the process would be slow. I followed her lead, since that was what she needed from me.

"It is now or never," Jackie was saying. "I'm almost turning 55, another big milestone. I've been thinking about my adoption. It's a big deal, you know. I was adopted as a child. I've decided, I need to find my biological parents."

I could understand the ambivalence Jackie had felt around doing so until now. Finding her biological parents would undoubtedly bring up a lot, and finding the right time and the right reason could be incredibly fraught. Now the time had arrived. I, of course, knew it wasn't going to be an exercise in box ticking; it was not 'something to get done', but it was perhaps understandable that it needed to be condensed down to that in Jackie's mind for her to manage the enormity of the task. Assuming Jackie was able to find and meet them, what happened next could splinter off into all kinds of different directions; it would never simply be 'done' or 'not done'. If all Jackie wanted was to find them, she could have hired a detective for this job, but perhaps, unconsciously, she was aware that she would need some support both before and after.

Jackie had previously mentioned she'd worked with a coach but ultimately chose to leave that relationship to explore finding her biological parents. I was curious why she had left.

"Did you feel you couldn't explore this with your coach?" I asked.

"He said he couldn't help me," Jackie responded.

Her answer sounded vague, deliberately so. What was the full story? I sensed there was more beneath the surface, but when I gently probed further, Jackie didn't elaborate. The conversation closed abruptly. She had a way of subtly shutting things down. A quiet but firm 'no entry' sign signalled that she was done talking. In those moments, I was left feeling disarmed, aware of the limits she set on emotional accessibility and the protectiveness that likely underpinned them.

After a short while, to my surprise, Jackie added, "I didn't like him much. He was humdrum. Silent. You know the sort. Boring."

I did wonder whether Jackie's silence was also met with a paralysis in the coach and I wondered why she sought a coach. Perhaps, on some level, Jackie did want help but not in the way she could easily name. Maybe she was searching for someone who could meet not just her words, but the parts of herself she usually kept suppressed. There is often a lot going on even in the silence. One's engagement is not only centred on the material but also the personality and presence of the therapist. I certainly would not describe myself as boring. Over the years, I have worked hard at breaking the mould of the 'blank slate' approach. This mould has been amazingly tough to shake off. But I've come to believe that allowing aspects of my own humanity into the room, appropriately, can help clients feel more met, more connected and more willing to engage on a deeper level.

"Anyway," Jackie resumed, clasping her hands. "We're here now. Do you know anything about adoption?"

Of course, I knew about adoption from my clinical work; I had written a book about it. It is an area close to my heart – the adoptees, adopted parents and local authorities. My hope was and is that more children would find adoptive parents who understand the intricacies around adoption. That adoption starts in grief. Understanding this foundation changes how we respond to behaviours and emotional challenges.

"I do have knowledge and experience of working with adoptees, and I'm here to support you in exploring whatever feels important to you about your experience."

"To be honest, I feel very alone in this journey?"

"Do your parents know you're embarking on this journey?"

"They won't understand?"

"Well, they think they've done a good job. Can't see the relevance..." After a long pause, she continued. "Anyway, I don't want to talk about them."

There was a long silence. I noted how Jackie controlled the therapy with these silences. The silence conveyed a closed chapter. It reminded me that in such moments, what is left unsaid can be as significant as what is spoken. The questions may be too confrontational. Therefore, rather than pressing further, I proactively shifted the lens and brought things to the present day.

Therapists juggle a few tasks at once. We are listening, thinking, reflecting and choosing what would be an appropriate interpretation and intervention, including silence. We use the tools we've been taught to give something back in response to what the client is putting to us.

Even though Jackie had come to me for help, she seemed unable or unwilling to engage. I, on the other hand, gradually began to feel a sense of lethargy and purposelessness over time. In one session, after a long period of silence and just a few weeks into our work, I decided to gently break the silence.

"Is there anything you feel comfortable sharing about yourself, work, family?" I asked, offering an open invitation rather than a direct demand, something to help her re-engage.

Jackie relaxed a bit. "I work at a retirement home with people over 60 who require assisted living."

I was surprised by this disclosure and wondered whether her choice of work–a setting defined by routine, relative inactivity and predictability–suited Jackie. It reminded me of how our sessions had been: muted and suspended in a kind of emotional haze; a daydream-like state, waiting for something, perhaps someone, to stir it awake.

"Tell me more," I said to prompt her on.

"Yes, I've been doing it for five years."

Now we were getting somewhere. Her words were still few, but they carried weight. I thought I had nothing to lose by probing a bit more. I continued with the line of questioning, although it felt somewhat instrumental and mechanical, very unlike how we've been trained to work. It was as if I had slipped into a role that felt more like an interviewer. Where this is okay at times, it shouldn't be the way to navigate therapy. I had to try something different before the conversation halted again.

"And how do you feel about your work?" I looked keenly at her. "I mean, working with the elderly. Do you like it?"

Jackie raised her brows and gave a short, dry laugh, then shrugged. "Oh, I don't like it. I feel it's pointless. Nothing is going to change for these folks because the home can't support them properly. We simply do our best to delay the inevitable."

I wondered how much this spoke to Jackie's own experience of life, a sense of pointlessness and doom.

"You sound disappointed. Why did you take the job?"

She inhaled slowly. "It was something I knew how to do, seeing as I helped my adopted parents in their old age."

"Can you tell me about that?"

Her eyes flicked to mine, then away. She folded her arms, suddenly more guarded. "Some other day."

I wasn't going to push any further. The calculated response said everything. It was too much for her to cope with. Nonetheless, Jackie continued turning up, and I assumed that something was working.

Some sessions later, she began in her usual manner, asking how I was. I replied that I was well and asked how she was. She said she was fine.

"I know the process is difficult," I said. "After all, you've already tried working with a coach. You must have been disappointed that it didn't work out so, I can understand why you might feel cautious about going through this again."

There was a slight smile of acknowledgement, or at least I thought there was. I wanted Jackie's trust and remained open to whatever difficult experiences might emerge, while respecting the many no-go areas. Questions were often met with hesitation and certain topics were deferred to a later, unspecified date. Jackie needed to be allowed the time she needed to open up.

About a year in, something began to soften. She started bringing more personal material like stand-out memories, opinions and even flashes of humour. One afternoon, almost offhandedly, she mentioned that her adoptive parents were white. Her adoptive mother had had a series of affairs and was often absent, both physically and emotionally. Her adoptive father was a quadriplegic, and Jackie felt closer to him. I wondered whether their differences, and the weight of their respective challenges, had made them more empathetic towards one another. Perhaps this created space for a kind of communication that felt more honest and more open. Then, during Jackie's teenage years, her mother decided to adopt another child.

"Do you think they adopted a second child to keep you company?" I asked, watching her face.

"No. It was because they simply could," Jackie replied, offering a composed smile.

I was taken aback by the bluntness. Her delivery was deadpan, stripped of sentiment. Beneath, I sensed exhaustion, detachment and a quiet anger she had learned to mute. Jackie's cynical outlook often surfaced in moments like this–a stark honesty that felt both revealing and guarded. She didn't embellish or soften her perspective to make others comfortable. It was as if she had long concluded that people in her life often acted not out of love or duty, but simply because they had the means, the impulse, or the power to do so.

I knew other white families who had adopted Black children. I also knew that adoption agencies generally try to keep a child within their birth family where possible and, if not, to place them with adoptive parents as close as possible to the child's ethnic background. Such proximity can make it easier for the adopted child to have their needs met. There is already enough for a child to contend with such as feelings of rejection or abandonment, without the added burden of navigating difference and belonging. Adoption agencies aim to give children the opportunity to grow up in a contained and stable home. However, racial identity must also be considered and embraced as integral to the child's sense of self.

Jackie remembered being a lonely child. She often felt like she was on display, like a showpiece her parents had acquired more for what she represented than for who she actually was. Her own wants and feelings were secondary to how she fit into their narrative. Her family was comfortable and lived in a mostly white village. Jackie described feeling conspicuous everywhere. She didn't give specific examples, but the way she spoke carried weight, as though this experience had shaped her entire sense of self. One could imagine her sitting quietly at dinner parties or walking through the village, acutely aware of every lingering glance.

She spoke very little about the village, other than expressing a strong desire never to return. Since her father's death, she had not found the courage to go back. Jackie described the home environment as 'complex'; that was the word she chose and delivered with careful neutrality. Then, without warning, her face crumpled and tears streamed down her cheeks. It caught me off guard, as did my own emotional response; at times, I found it difficult not to join in her tears.

I wondered what had shifted. Perhaps speaking about the village, her father, and that complex home had stirred grief that had never been expressed. When left alone as a child, Jackie played with her dolls, imagining them as part of a family she had created. In that imaginary world, she controlled the rules, the tone and the outcomes. Her dolls were not just toys; they were stand-ins for the emotional connection she longed for but did not receive.

Jackie's adoptive mother tried to introduce various activities, but this felt too little too late. The neglect had already taken its toll. By the age of 14, Jackie was dying to leave home. In her youth, Jackie befriended a much older man she described as charismatic. What she believed was a relationship was, in reality, an emotional entanglement born out of need and inexperience. Perhaps she saw in him the protective father she had wished for – someone older, attentive and seemingly caring. But the protection she sought became something far more dangerous. He abused her trust, gradually introducing her to other men and to drugs. Jackie naïvely believed this was normal. This marked the beginning of multiple stints in and out of rehabilitation.

"Looking back," I asked, "how do you feel about the choices you were being asked to make then? Did you get what you wanted, or was it all about him?"

She hesitated. "At first, I didn't really think about it. It just felt like that was what we were supposed to do. I didn't feel like I had a choice. He made it seem like this was normal–like this was what being grown up, or loved, meant."

By this point, Jackie had started to be more open with me. She had shared memories of loneliness, abuse and addiction. But when it came to her adoptive mother, there was a wall. Their relationship, she said, had fractured years ago. She offered this information plainly and refused to elaborate. It was clear this was the one part of her story she would not touch. We left it there, unspoken but heavy, like a closed door she was not ready, or willing, to open.

Keeping in mind the project Jackie had come to therapy for, I checked in about her search for her biological family. I thought that achieving her primary goal might offer some stability, that one positive anchor amid so much distress.

"It's taking longer than I thought," she said, her tone neutral, though there was a flicker of something I couldn't quite put my finger on.

I found myself wondering whether the search was about more than biology. After everything she had endured–the neglect, the abuse, and the failed attempt to find safety in an older partner who exploited her–perhaps the search carried a deeper hope: of being chosen, seen and claimed. A kind of rescue. But, she offered nothing further.

Days and weeks passed. We sat in long silences. I asked about her thoughts; she responded with work-related details or neutral facts. Then silence returned. Over time, the silences became attuned. We were witnessing something unnamed but deeply felt. There was, paradoxically, a restful sense of being together. Gradually, a common theme emerged: Jackie had moved through much of her life unseen. Her adoptive family had met her basic needs but without curiosity or emotional engagement.

"They must have loved me," she said quietly one afternoon, as though trying to convince herself. "Otherwise, why adopt me?"

Yet in another session, her tone sharpened. "They never asked me anything. Not about how I felt. It was like I was a project they'd finished and didn't want to revisit."

That tension–between hope and hurt, longing and anger–ran through much of her narrative. In the family's disregard for what made Jackie unique, she often felt like the odd one out and hated herself for it. Secretly, she wished she were white. This was a painful but understandable revelation. She had no role models offering a positive reflection of herself; even the popular culture consumed by the family favoured images that resembled them, not her. As her identity was not celebrated, Jackie struggled to develop a full sense of self. I often wondered whether her choice of a Black female therapist was, unconsciously, a step towards repair.

For a Black child, racial identity should be affirmed and celebrated, particularly in environments where they are minoritised. Difference is often stigmatised, yet it need not divide us. White children rarely need to think about their race; it is treated as the norm. Black children, however, are made aware of their difference early on – sometimes subtly, sometimes explicitly. For Jackie, this awareness was deeply felt, even if never spoken. For adoptees, there is an added layer: the experience of having been given up. Jackie's adoptive mother might have helped by positively affirming her difference, reducing feelings of alienation rather than reinforcing them.

In early adulthood, following the abusive relationship, Jackie's resignation took riskier forms. She described having little regard for safety or even for life itself. Drugs offered both numbness and belonging. Among others who felt displaced, she found a sense of family. Life during that period felt transitory; people, places, time itself passing without anchor. That changed when she decided to adopt a little girl. It was a decision that surprised even her. For the first time, someone needed her, not because she was useful, but because she had chosen to be their parent.

"What changed?" I asked once.

"It wasn't about me anymore," she said. "I didn't want her to feel what I'd felt, like she didn't matter."

Her daughter became her centre. However, she was later diagnosed with attention deficit disorder (ADD) and autism spectrum disorder (ASD). ADD involves difficulties with attention, focus and impulsivity, while ASD is associated with differences in social communication, sensory processing and emotional regulation. Jackie spoke of sleepless nights, fear and dysregulation, and of moments when she worried that she might harm her child. Yet despite this, mother and daughter found ways to connect. Parenting became Jackie's way of breaking intergenerational cycles of trauma, neglect and addiction.

"The agent found my uncle, my father's brother. Not what I expected but he is keen to get in touch!"

She was ecstatic, grinning ear to ear. This was a new smile and for the first time in a year, Jackie regained some liveliness, even though the agent had confirmed that her mother was dead.

"Not the news you hoped for."

"No but what can I do? I'm hoping he'll have news of my father... I hope it will be good news..." She trailed off and I could hear the anxiety in her voice. "We'll have to wait and see," she sighed.

Several sessions later, Jackie reported that she had met her uncle who had been thrilled to meet her. Sadly, she found out that her father had also died. Nevertheless, Jackie was not as affected as she could have been, and she justified it by saying that she never knew him, anyway. I wondered whether these losses would be later realised. It turned out that her uncle had known about her all along and had always wanted to find her too. It seems that things progressed quite quickly from that initial reunion and plans were made to introduce her to the rest of the family in Cape Town.

I felt there was still important work to be done: managing losses, addressing long-standing patterns and helping her consolidate a more stable sense of self. Yet I understood her need to try something new. Remaining in therapy might have kept her tethered to the past she was trying to leave behind. She knew she could return.

Some might have called this a 'flight to health.' I had anticipated it. Cape Town offered possibility and a place where she might not feel othered. It was impossible to know what lay ahead. My hope was that this new chapter would be a positive and transformative one.

Jackie presented with a clear goal: to locate her biological parents. While this focus demonstrated motivation, it also functioned as a defence, allowing her to manage anxiety, maintain control and limit vulnerability. Her guarded persona, which was made up of strategic silences, minimal disclosure and careful regulation of emotion–reflected both her adoption history and experiences of neglect, early trauma and racial marginalisation.

Winnicott's concept of play helped frame the therapeutic approach. Jackie had limited capacity for emotional spontaneity, likely shaped by environments where feelings were dismissed or policed. Therapy required creating a space that tolerated silence and respected boundaries, gradually inviting engagement and reflection.

Over time, Jackie began to explore complex experiences: her adoptive family relationships, racial identity, past abuse and parenting her neurodivergent daughter. Her search for her biological parents became symbolic of a deeper need to be seen, chosen and validated.

Clinically, the case highlighted the importance of patience, attunement, and flexibility. Supporting clients with strong defence mechanisms requires balancing containment with gentle challenge and fostering relational safety. Jackie's gradual progress, as evidenced by incremental disclosure, reflection on intergenerational patterns and readiness for a new chapter, demonstrates the potential for meaningful change when therapy holds both vulnerability and resilience.

Leah: Navigating Motherhood and Silence

When I was training, there was not much conversation around the dynamic between a white therapist and a Black client, and even less about the reverse. The general idea was that we were all the same, and therefore the focus should be on the internal world. This idea would work seamlessly if we lived in a perfect world where things were equal for everyone. However, upon reflection, this approach seems more likely rooted in how to turn a blind eye.

Saying "I'm Black and you're white" is just naming a binary, but what truly informs the therapeutic dynamic are the historical, social and systemic realities embedded in those identities. Ignoring that context risks missing key layers of meaning, trust, power and trauma that shape the client's internal world and their relationship to the therapist.

I've shown how much therapeutic work can be enriched when we acknowledge race in the consulting room and the feelings it generates. The impact of racism–widespread colonisation, the legacy of slavery and generational transmission–is profound. I am calling for more honest engagement with the racial and cultural realities that shape both client and therapist engagement.

Problems arise in psychoanalysis when the white majority ignores race. To make matters worse, the theoretical edifice of psychoanalysis has been built upon a white, middle-class approach, largely excluding the non-white experience.

When a Black therapist in the Western world works with a white client, the therapist is often more familiar with the cultural context and social norms of that client's environment because they navigate that society daily. Even though their racial identities differ, their socialisation and lived experiences in the same cultural setting can provide a degree of shared understanding.

By contrast, when a white therapist works with a Black client who is new to that Western context, the therapist may have limited exposure to the client's cultural background. In some cases, the therapist may encounter someone from a Black culture for the first time in the therapy room, making it harder to intuitively understand the client's lived realities shaped by history, migration or systemic factors.

When a white client works with a Black therapist, they may bring conscious and unconscious biases and projections into the therapeutic relationship, shaped by societal narratives and racialised stereotypes such as assumptions about authority, competence, emotional resilience, threat or caretaking. These stereotypes are historically rooted in colonial and racial hierarchies and may surface subtly through doubt, idealisation, defensiveness or unconscious testing of the therapist's role and expertise. Therefore, it is essential to acknowledge what lies behind these projections from either party. Doing so allows for a more authentic, honest and healing therapeutic relationship that considers the impact of race, power and history.

"Can you tell me what's brought you here?"

"I feel stuck in a rut," Leah answered, a Caucasian woman who looked to be in her 30s.

"Stuck?"

"Yes. I feel depressed."

"Depressed? Is this a new feeling?"

"No, I feel this most of the time."

I remained quiet for a moment, allowing space for reflection. Leah had a slightly shy, modest demeanour, constantly adjusting her glasses and sitting very primly. She was dressed stylishly but not ostentatiously. There was a subtle discomfort about her, as if she felt hesitant to take up space. She seemed apologetic and somewhat timid.

"I'm somewhat apathetic. I'm just going through the motions day-to-day, but don't feel like I ever actually choose to do anything. I guess I don't quite belong anywhere. I want to find my place in the world."

We began working together in autumn 2018. What would unfold over the next three years was a gradual process of Leah learning to take up space–first in the therapy room, and eventually in her life. The organisation I worked for at the time had matched us. I didn't have an online profile then, and my name gave no indication of my cultural heritage. Leah more than likely expected a white therapist. Even though I am familiar with working with both white and Black clients, I often sense a different metaphorical bridge to cross with white clients. After all, Black people are more frequently perceived as less knowledgeable, less professional and less valued. This position has been internalised, to varying degrees, by both races through a value system in which Black people often look to white people for help. Here, the roles were reversed.

Therapeutic work is often enriched by clarifying what is feared to be happening and what is taking place in the therapeutic relationship. Unexamined fears, frequently rooted in past relational experiences or internalised assumptions, can shape perception and expectation, obscuring the reality of the present encounter. While it may not have been immediately obvious, this underlying issue loomed over our first session.

"Can you help me?" Leah asked apprehensively.

There was something in how she asked, tentatively, almost apologetically, that made me wonder if she was questioning not just whether therapy could help, but whether I, specifically, could help her. The unspoken question hung between us: could a Black therapist understand the experiences of a white client?

This dynamic of a Black therapist working with a white client remains relatively uncommon and carries its own complexities. I was acutely aware that Leah might be wondering about my competence, my authority or my ability to understand her world. These doubts, often unconscious, are shaped by societal narratives about who holds knowledge, who has authority and who is qualified to guide others towards healing.

At the same time, I noticed my own responses. I felt a particular pressure to prove myself competent, to demonstrate that I could help her and to earn her trust in ways that went beyond the usual therapeutic process. This pressure, I recognised, was not just about being a good therapist; it was about being a Black therapist working with a white client in a field that has historically been dominated by white practitioners working with white clients.

"It sounds like you are feeling disconnected from a sense of purpose or direction," I responded.

I thought about how lonely this place would feel for Leah. This is a familiar question for clients who come to therapy, regardless of the therapist. Wanting to find one's place in the world is a core human drive. In our scenario, we were also grappling with the prescriptive meaning behind race.

"Honestly, Abi, I sometimes feel like I'm just making a fuss about nothing. There are so many people with much bigger problems than mine. There's a part of me that feels guilty about bringing all these stupid, tiny little first-world problems to you. There's nothing wrong, really. When I hear myself saying, 'I'm not sure who I am,' it makes me cringe."

When Leah referred to her difficulties as 'first-world problems', it seemed to reveal an unspoken concern about how I might see her. Because I am Black, she may have assumed that I would view her struggles–questions about identity and meaning as trivial compared to what she imagined I, or others like me, might have faced. In that moment, I understood something important about what was happening between us. Leah was trying to position her suffering as less valid than what she imagined mine, or other Black people's might be. This comparison, while perhaps well-intentioned, created a barrier. It suggested that only certain kinds of pain counted, that her internal struggles were somehow frivolous because they weren't about survival or systemic oppression.

But suffering isn't a competition. Depression doesn't care about privilege. The sense of not knowing who you are or where you belong; these are fundamentally human struggles, not the exclusive domain of any particular group. What Leah needed to understand was that her pain was real and deserved attention, not because it was comparable to anyone else's, but because it was hers.

I also recognised that her assumption, which was that I might view her problems as trivial, revealed something about how race was operating in our relationship. She saw me as someone who had faced real hardship and therefore might judge her for struggling with questions of identity and purpose. This projection, while unconscious, shaped how she presented herself to me: apologetic, minimising and careful not to take up too much space.

What she perhaps didn't realise was that I, as her therapist, was familiar with navigating predominantly white spaces, understanding white culture and working within systems designed primarily for white people. I had spent my entire professional life developing cultural competence in her world. The question wasn't whether I could understand her; it was whether she could allow herself to be fully seen by me.

By downplaying her own pain, Leah was trying to protect herself from possible judgment and the fear of appearing self-absorbed or ungrateful. This reflects a wider social idea that some forms of suffering count more than others, and that people from certain backgrounds are expected to be more resilient or less affected by inner struggles. In therapy, these assumptions can quietly get in the way. If they are not brought into the open, they can stop people from speaking honestly about what they are going through. By gently addressing the difference between what Leah feared I might think and what was actually happening between us, we were able to return to what mattered most–her experience, which was real and deserving of attention.

Both the racial assumption and the projection reveal the complex, often unconscious ways race and power shape the therapeutic relationship. For every interaction, the client is searching to be truly seen. The Black-white binary adds a particular layer to this dynamic, a challenge of colour as a category that, in itself, is empty but heavily loaded with meaning.

Getting to know a client depends on discovering commonalities, building trust, fostering respect and even genuinely liking the person. As with any therapeutic relationship, there is always much more happening beneath the surface than what is spoken aloud. I found myself drawn to Leah, and I believe that connection helps. Of course, the outcome of any therapy is impossible to predict. What we create together emerges through collaboration and a mutual willingness: a wish to be known and a wish to know.

"I do wonder whether you're also wondering about our compatibility. After all, we look different. And that difference can carry meaning, even if it's not easy to put into words."

Leah nodded somewhat uncomfortably.

"If your problems are important to you, they are important to me," I continued.

Leah relaxed a little after that. She needed to know her problems, which she labelled as being trivial, were in fact important to her and, hopefully, to me. She was seeking confirmation and trying to find a way to relate to me.

"So, tell me more about yourself," I asked with a genuine curiosity.

Leah was in her 30s and was an only child. She was renting an apartment above a public house and had lived there for some years. She didn't have a presence in the place – no pictures on the walls and she didn't own the furniture. Leah felt like she was living in a borrowed space. Her father, who ran the pub, constantly intruded on her personal space, symbolising how his authority and expectations deeply permeated Leah's life, leaving her little room for privacy or independence. Superficially, this is what she meant by not really belonging. On a deeper level, she was questioning belonging anywhere, including even in therapy. Leah wanted to be liked, which for her meant not inconveniencing others. There was a sort of bargain in her head – if she was agreeable, people would like her. She lived within the confines of what others needed and wanted.

Her friendly, punctual and pleasant nature made her an ideal client in some ways. I felt genuine warmth toward her. Yet in those early days, it was difficult to grasp who she really was and what she truly wanted. She appeared to lack confidence, but the problem was deeper than that. When we spoke, I could sense that she was wrestling with traits about herself that she deemed unacceptable. In the therapy space, she kept herself small, neither vocalising needs nor expressing desires, careful not to cause any trouble. I felt a strong maternal transference towards her, sensing she was someone who needed protecting. I got the impression that at some point, she had been forced to feel as though she wasn't allowed to have any demands. Therefore, she seemed to move through life as someone well-practised in curbing her own personality.

At times, Leah said she felt furious with herself when she'd said or done the wrong thing. She was always surprised by these feelings, baffled as to where such intense rage came from. It highlighted a disconnect between her conscious awareness and her deeper emotional currents. It felt as if she had to be so vigilant and controlled about her emotions that she had internalised and suppressed a lot of her feelings over the years. The result was a build-up of intense emotions, like rage, that surfaced unexpectedly and felt alien or confusing to her.

Nurturing a child's needs and wants can be a challenge for many parents. Often, children who are non-compliant are considered demanding, when in fact it is the overly compliant child we also need to worry about. The concern is often rooted in what they are trying to fend off to be agreeable. For Leah, being compliant meant suppressing her own needs and feelings to avoid conflict. It was a way of protecting herself by staying quiet and agreeable, even when it cost her a sense of authenticity and self-expression. Perhaps this was part of Leah's early experience. When points of difference are avoided or suppressed in early development, when uniqueness is met with discomfort rather than curiosity, something essential is lost; not only is self-expression stifled, but so is the capacity to be curious about the other. This curiosity is crucial for developing empathy, understanding and meaningful connection across difference. How children are nurtured around their unique traits can shape how prepared they are to engage with the wider world, cultures and ideas different from their own.

Nurturing a child's unique character allows them to welcome difference in themselves and fosters curiosity about others. When parents consistently discourage a child's curiosity about people or cultures outside their experience – often because these perspectives are unfamiliar – they are not only passing down a limited worldview but also inhibiting the child's natural curiosity. This shapes not only how the child sees themselves but also how much of the world they allow themselves to be open to.

In a world adjusting to increased migration, this feels like a vital part of raising children, but it is often overlooked. Many white people live within predominantly white neighbourhoods and may never come across people of colour in their lifetime. In contrast, Black people consciously and unconsciously try to assimilate, seeking proximity to whiteness in order to climb social ladders and gain a sense of belonging. In doing so, they may tone down or give up parts of their cultural identity. This is a great loss, as a wealth of culture is sacrificed in the pursuit of belonging. There is so much pull towards and cohesion with whiteness that any attempt at separateness is shunned and pathologised for not being the norm.

During my experience teaching a module called 'Difference and Diversity' on my psychotherapy postgraduate training, I was often asked why there was such a focus on race. Trainees who carried invisible differences, such as being Irish or working-class, felt as though their differences were not considered important. The short answer is that visible differences carry a layer of projection. Colour is a signifier, and the negativity ascribed to colour is often denied. What does this denial serve? Denying colour whitewashes difference in the therapeutic dyad. This is not to say that other differences are unimportant, nor that any form of othering is significant. But the added layer of race and racism in the client's sense of self and belonging represents a crucial difference that cannot be ignored. Cultural differences, as well as gender, sexuality and social class, are intertwined and complex. They shape how we navigate our existence. Ultimately, the hope for anyone coming to therapy is that we can reach them in a way that makes them feel seen. As I said to Leah, if your problems are important to you, they are important to me.

Leah's lack of confidence was also influenced by her mother dying when Leah was ten. Without a mother figure, Leah navigated life largely on her own and this was compounded by the fact that she was an only child. I could easily empathise with her feelings. Her mother had been ill for a while with a degenerative disease, and Leah had witnessed her suffering. As a family, they had tried various remedies, including travelling overseas for treatment, but nothing seemed to help.

When her mother could no longer work and her illness worsened, Leah would often stay by her bedside, attentive to her needs. Their relationship had been close. Leah had been an adaptive child, complying with whatever was asked; she could not go against the grain. Before her illness, Leah described how her mother had been too busy working to spend time with her. Now that she was gone, Leah admitted regretting their moments apart and felt a sadness that she couldn't keep her mother alive. Her death left a significant gap in Leah's life. The pain of that loss preceded a sense of hopelessness and helplessness. That deep sense of loss and separation led to a fear of further loss, keeping her stuck in jobs and relationships, often anxious about change. The grief had anchored her in place even as life moved forwards.

After her mother died, her father immersed himself in work and became more socially dependent on Leah, leaning on her for emotional support, conversation and companionship. She became the person he confided in, filling the emotional void left by his wife. Not long after, her father began a relationship with another woman and, less than a year later, moved in with her. He then sold the family home. The speed of these changes, coupled with the loss of the place where so many memories lived, left Leah feeling abandoned and betrayed. She held a deep resentment towards her father.

As an adult, Leah worked as a paramedic. I was struck by her wish to save lives, but also her desire to stay within acceptable boundaries. She had a degree in medicine but didn't want to progress further or take on more responsibilities. Fearing failure, Leah felt like an imposter at her job. She had initially pursued medicine largely to please her father and from a desire to do the right thing. She was competent and content to support patients as required, though uninterested in self-promotion. She remained gripped by fear of making mistakes–any error felt catastrophic.

Leah had also dated occasionally, including an affair at work that gradually faded. Soon after, she began a relationship with another man, Alan. Like her father, he worked long hours. Leah admired his dedication, as it felt familiar and steady. He had a strong 'alpha male' presence, someone who provided, organised and managed aspects of her life. Emotional connection, however, was limited; support was shown through actions rather than understanding or empathy. When they went out, he was often surrounded by female friends and would leave her for periods of time. Leah felt envious of his relationships with other women and felt she had to compete for his attention.

"He says he can't talk to me in the same way he does with his friends, his female friends that is. He's always had female friends, and they have this kind of bond. That's what he calls it.

Apparently, what we have is different. But why? Why can't he even include me in those conversations? I'm not going to force my way in, but it'd be nice to be asked."

I wasn't sure about this behaviour. I suspected he might be having an affair. I raised this with her. Leah doubted it, yet something in her tone suggested uncertainty. I felt protective of her while also concerned about why she was accommodating such behaviour. Leah's reluctance to 'rock the boat' reflected a pattern of accepting situations that undermined her. This quiet resignation had the potential to chip away at her confidence. Leah needed to face the possibility of a different life, one not dependent on the approval or presence of others but on her own agency.

The same people-pleasing behaviour played out at her workplace. Leah often felt overwhelmed, unable to say 'no' even when at capacity. She would rage at herself for being roped into tasks outside her responsibility, yet taking extra work also reflected ambition. Not wanting to rock the boat made sense. Leah had repressed much of her emotion in childhood and throughout life. As our sessions progressed, I felt as though I was 'holding the baby,' preserving her sense of self while absorbing and soothing her anxiety.

At times, her agreeable nature frustrated me. I assumed there was transference as she was often frustrated with herself. Leah had a lot of pent-up, self-directed anger, which erupted unexpectedly. Her rage suggested dissatisfaction with the life she had created. More than anything, she was looking for guidance. The consistency and regularity of our sessions offered a place to feel safe and in time, to explore possibilities rather than remaining stuck for fear of rejection.

Around 14 months into our work, a pivotal event occurred. Leah asked to shift our session time, explaining that her work schedule had changed. Without thinking it through carefully, I agreed immediately, wanting to accommodate her. The following week, because of an administrative error on my part, I missed our appointment. Leah therefore arrived at an empty consulting room. When I realised my mistake, I felt a complex mix of emotions: guilt for letting her down, but also recognition that something significant had just happened. My inability to say no to her request had inadvertently created a rupture that mirrored Leah's own patterns.

In our next session, I had to consider this slip in the therapeutic context carefully. My over-accommodation had inadvertently re-enacted something familiar to Leah – the pattern of agreeing to things that didn't really work, then failing to show up fully. Was this what it was like for her, constantly bending to others' needs until something gave way? I should have maintained my boundary from the start; doing so would have been beneficial long-term. Yet the mistake offered an invaluable opportunity for Leah to express frustration and disappointment, which were feelings she had spent a lifetime suppressing.

I began by acknowledging what had happened. "Leah, I want to address what happened last week. I made a mistake, first by agreeing to a time that didn't work well for me, and then by not being there when you arrived. I'm very sorry. I'm wondering how that was for you."

"Well, as you can imagine, I was a bit angry and upset. I was disappointed you weren't there. It takes me an hour to get here, so it felt like a waste of my time. I could have done something else."

Her tone was measured, but I could hear the hurt underneath. What struck me most was that she was expressing rather than minimising it, not making excuses for me and not immediately reassuring me that it was fine.

"You have every right to feel angry and disappointed," I said. "I let you down. And I'm glad you're telling me how it felt, rather than brushing it aside."

Leah looked surprised, as if she'd expected me to become defensive or to dismiss her feelings. "I thought you might think I was being dramatic," she said quietly.

"Not at all. Your feelings make complete sense. I wonder if this might connect to other times in your life when people haven't shown up for you in the way you needed them to."

Leah was quiet for a moment. Then she nodded slowly. "My father," she said. "After my mother died, he was physically there, but emotionally... he wasn't really present. And then he just moved on so quickly, as if she, and I, didn't matter."

That moment marked an important shift. Leah's willingness to express anger directly, to hold me accountable without fearing that our relationship would end, demonstrated a growing capacity to assert herself. Through this 'negative transference', which is the unconscious redirection of emotions from earlier relationships onto the therapist, meant that her feelings of anger, disappointment and frustration could be acknowledged and validated. It was important for her to realise that being angry was okay, that relationships could withstand conflict. Experiencing that her anger did not threaten our arrangement helped her see she could assert herself safely. More importantly, she had experienced something new: expressing disappointment and anger without being abandoned, dismissed or punished. I hadn't become defensive or made excuses. I had taken responsibility, apologised and remained present with her discomfort. This, perhaps more than anything we'd talked about in previous sessions, began to shift something fundamental to how Leah related to others.

Leah tended to avoid confrontation, including with her partner. She would compromise her boundaries to avoid losing him. Her mask of cordiality prevented the closeness she wanted. Her partner was often unavailable when out with friends, and we explored the connection to her experiences with her father, who leaned on her for emotional support after her mother's death. Leah had taken on her mother's role, bolstering her father's fragile ego and fearing loss. This same fear underpinned her current relationship: acknowledging her needs might risk losing her partner. We shared this realisation in silence. Leah sobbed quietly, recognising something long buried and allowing herself space to feel rather than speak.

"I was wondering. What do you do for yourself?" I gently asked.

"Well, I like cooking for Alan," she answered.

"Do you remember things you enjoyed before you met him? What would you do for yourself?"

"I used to like cycling," she said. "Cross-country. On a mountain bike. When I'm in nature, I feel so alive."

Cycling? I had not heard this before. "I wonder why you stopped."

"Not sure. Maybe we moved house. I hadn't thought about it before." Leah paused, hearing herself for the first time. "It's interesting. I should explore that."

Over time, Leah began reclaiming her sense of agency. She returned to cycling, which she had enjoyed before, rediscovering the physical and mental benefits. She also returned to reading, alternating these activities during her morning train commute.

Around two and a half years into our work, a managerial position opened at the hospital. Encouraged to apply, Leah applied and was offered the role. This created a dilemma: extra responsibility versus fear of failure. She eventually decided to accept the role for a year and return to her previous position if it didn't work out.

Therapy supported her in reframing failure as experimentation–trial and error was part of living. She embraced the role, surprised by the fact that she enjoyed the responsibility. Reading remained an escape, but gradually her confidence grew. Leah realised that being responsible at work was not enough; her self-esteem demanded more. She began asserting herself in her relationship, confronting her partner about exclusion and lack of respect. These small acts reinforced her sense of agency and self-worth. Later, Leah chose to retrain professionally, moving from medicine to a position as a business manager at an international laboratory warehouse. Choosing her own path allowed her to reclaim agency over her life, rather than living to please others.

By late 2021, nearly three years after we'd met, we agreed to begin working towards ending therapy. The long commute was making sessions unsustainable, and more importantly, Leah had reached a place where she felt ready. At the penultimate session, Leah mentioned her boss was an older Black woman; it was an interesting parallel, perhaps a symbolic transfer of guidance and affirmation into her life. It felt like a good conclusion to our work. I felt protective and deeply affectionate towards Leah, and I suspect she sensed that. We worked well together, and Leah remained in my thoughts for many years after therapy ended. There is more to connection than what is visible and spoken.

Working with Leah over three years taught me important lessons about the subtle ways early loss and family dynamics shape how we move through the world. Leah had learned early that taking up space, expressing needs or showing disappointment could lead to loss. Her mother had died, her father had emotionally withdrawn and then literally moved on, and Leah had internalised the belief that her survival depended on being agreeable, undemanding and small.

What struck me most about our work was how race operated as both a visible and invisible factor in our relationship. Leah had expected a white therapist – someone who looked like her, whose authority felt natural and unquestioned. Instead, she found me. And while she never said so directly, I sensed her initial uncertainty: could a Black woman therapist understand her world? Did I have the competence, the training or the cultural knowledge to help someone like her? These questions, largely unconscious, shaped our early sessions. Leah was exceedingly polite, careful and apologetic – not just because that was her personality, but because she was navigating an unfamiliar power dynamic. In the broader world, white people often hold authority and Black people are positioned as those who serve, support or accommodate. In our therapy room, that dynamic was reversed, and it created a particular kind of tension.

I noticed my own responses, too. I felt a pressure to prove myself, to demonstrate competence, to earn her trust in ways that went beyond the usual therapeutic process. This wasn't just about being a good therapist; it was about being a Black therapist in a field where Black practitioners are still seen as the exception rather than the norm. I wanted Leah to benefit from the work, not just for her sake, but as proof that I belonged in this role.

The moment when Leah described her problems as first-world problems was particularly revealing. She was trying to position her suffering as less valid than what she imagined mine might be–a comparison rooted in assumptions about race and hardship. But this comparison created a barrier. It suggested that only certain kinds of pain counted, that her internal struggles were somehow frivolous because they weren't about survival or systemic oppression.

Kay: Intersectionality and Self-Recognition

I have my own thoughts about clients before I meet them, and the same is true for the client about me. Clients are often anxious when they start therapy. There is an element of entering an unknown space, yet an opportunity for discovery. Therapy is a space of frustration and grappling, but also of joy, insight and revelation. What a client comes for may not be what they leave with; all they know is that they want to feel better. With so many variables at play, assumptions are often made before the client-therapist relationship even begins. It's a way of having something to hold on to.

A therapist's pre-transference refers to the feelings and thoughts they may have before meeting a client. This can include assumptions about how the client arrives, who is paying or even the tone of an email. Such cues subtly shape expectations and offer hints about how the process might unfold. However, we are trained to approach therapy without preconceptions, open to what the client brings. But we are human. Early impressions often reflect our own countertransference–feelings stirred up by something about the client or the situation.

Kay had emailed to request an appointment, mentioning difficulties in her romantic relationship but offering few details. From her brief email, I sensed a certain guardedness, an emotional distance, as if she were unsure about reaching out for help. This carried over into our first session. Kay was incredibly quiet, observing me carefully while maintaining a polished and accomplished exterior.

During the first session, I asked whether she had any questions. I expected questions about therapy, but instead she asked where I was from. Initially, this threw me. My credentials weren't uppermost in my mind and her question seemed to prioritise my background over my professional role. After a pause, I decided to answer directly.

"I was born in Nigeria."

Kay looked surprised. "I wouldn't have thought that."

I paused, unsure of how to respond. Kay herself was Black British, of Ghanaian descent. She knew I was Black, but not my specific background. I chose not to probe her remark further, sensing that doing so might irritate her.

"I thought you were from Jamaica," she laughed. "If you were, I'm not sure our interaction would have worked. We are culturally quite different. Africans don't often bother with therapy; we know where we come from."

"But you've come for therapy," I countered gently. "There's something that's brought you here."

Kay didn't respond.

In social discourse, a cultural divide often exists between Black people from Africa and the Caribbean, despite the shared African heritage. This divide has historical roots in slavery and colonisation. I sensed Kay was a little sceptical, both of me and of therapy. Seeking help is rarely a neutral act; it implies that control has been lost somewhere. I understood the taboo surrounding therapy in many Black communities. Internalized beliefs and historical realities such as misdiagnosis, under-treatment and systemic prejudice have made therapy untrustworthy to some. Internalising dominant cultural narratives can distort self-perception and reinforce cycles of oppression, where feelings of inferiority and superiority play out in everyday relationships.

Kay sized me up, yet she also waited for my lead.

"Tell me about you," I prompted.

"I'm a restaurant manager," she replied.

"And what drew you to this work?"

"I'm organised and methodical. I have an 11-person team reporting to me. They're exceptional. I like my team and they like me too. I mean, why wouldn't they?" Kay laughed.

She came across as confident at work having been in the role for years, was task-oriented, efficient and in control. Yet, delving deeper revealed complexities in her family background. She was the youngest of three, with older brothers who were dominant. Growing up, she felt overshadowed and excluded.

"They would exclude me," she said. "They'd be out playing volleyball or doing something else, but I wasn't allowed to participate. You'd think being the youngest, I'd be spoiled. But it was the complete opposite."

"What about your relationship with your mother?" I asked.

Kay frowned. "We never really got along. There was distance. I couldn't understand why. She wasn't affectionate. I don't think she knew what to do with me."

She continued, describing her family in fragmented pieces. Her mother had shared little of her own past, and the household had been structured around expectations rather than emotional connection. Achievement, particularly academic, was prioritised over personal fulfilment. Kay's mother, like many African mothers, wanted her children to succeed financially and socially, ensuring a life free from hardship. The children were rarely given autonomy in their choices; their worth was tied to achievement rather than personal satisfaction.

Kay now had little contact with her family. She noted that her upbringing reflected broader historical patterns rooted in post-slavery migration, displacement and family fracturing; these factors disproportionately affected Black women. They were expected to hold families together and care for others, often denying themselves support. These inherited patterns created deep emotional marks: unresolved grief, ruptures in connection and sacrifices passed down through generations. Kay's current disconnection existed within these broader currents of history, race, gender and survival.

"So, we grew up together, but I wouldn't say we were close," she reflected. "Family history, who our ancestors were, where they came from... no information. It made me wonder whether my parents wanted to detach from their own family. Family, to them, always spelled problems."

Kay's father didn't feature in her narrative, only her stepfather. She described her mother as subdued in the household, while her stepfather wielded authority. Yet she respected him for the effort and expense he put into raising them in the UK.

When her parents met her boyfriend, they approved, describing him as suitable. Over time, however, delays in commitment and an expectation that Kay play the dutiful partner created frustration. She resented being the sole homemaker despite working full-time. This mirrored her mother's own experience of subservience in her marriage, teaching Kay to tolerate situations she did not desire.

Initially, I couldn't understand why Kay tolerated this. She was financially independent and successful. I discovered that her boyfriend's generosity, combined with her own income, created a comfortable lifestyle, which contributed to a sense of obligation–a subtle *quid pro quo*. Kay masked the confusion, displacement and devaluation that was going on internally.

I was always surprised by the way she dramatically entered my room. On the surface, she radiated confidence. She would be dressed for work, showing up in expensive, formal clothes with matching shoes. Then she draped her long coat on a chair in a way that suggested that she liked drawing attention to her expensive items in a bid to provoke envy and, as a mask to the vulnerability she felt within.

These appearances made a stark contrast to the woman described at home. It was this split between the successful woman in the workplace and the cowed, silent housekeeper at home that had brought her to therapy; she wanted to shed something of the timidity and be more confident in vocalising her feelings. My task was to help heal the split by bringing this dissonance to her awareness, then work towards helping her regain a sense of control over all aspects of her life. Kay didn't understand why she subjected herself to an unhappy life at home yet saw no way out.

"I can see that your partner is generous with money. But from what you've told me, you make more than enough by yourself."

"It's not just that," Kay responded.

It seems that Kay was holding out for marriage and the vision of starting a family. She wanted to get married and felt it shaming to have been engaged for so long. Kay had invested so much time with him, ten years to be exact, and she wasn't giving that up.

"I'm not going to get anyone better. There is no Mr. Right who has everything you want. I need to compromise, so I'm sticking with him."

Even though Kay wasn't prepared to risk any change, I felt hopeful as she kept on coming to her appointments.

I was sitting with so much of her frustration when one day I asked: "Could your partner change and become a man who respects you in the way you need?"

She paused. "Maybe. No, I'm not sure."

Being controlled in this way is what Kay had known all her life. It was this change that Kay had come for, which was also resisted. If Kay was less fearful of loss, she might have found the courage to assert her needs–perhaps even to push for more shared responsibility at home, making it clear how important that was to her. My thought process was to gently guide her towards recognising her own agency. If Kay saw herself differently and related to that self differently, she would have found herself in a place where pursuing her own dreams was possible. But as time went by, a couple of years in fact, I felt continued frustration at the inertia of not getting anywhere; Kay was similarly frustrated with herself. She felt stuck and unable to bring about the change she longed for.

Some people have therapy to support them in navigating a chosen path. Most, however, seek change. They catch glimpses of what life could be like, but it is as if they're tethered to their suffering, almost addicted to it and fear the unknowns that freedom may bring. Change caries risk and for many it is easier to cling to the familiar.

It's important not just to notice resistance; it's crucial to understand what that resistance is about and what it might be protecting. For Kay, this resistance was about self-protection, which kept her in the safety of the familiar. It was not for me to tell Kay, or any of my clients, what to do, however.

The purpose of therapy is to help individuals be more attuned to their ego-self and less dominated by the superego. The superego is the internalised voices of parents, authority figures and societal expectations. As we strengthen the connection to the ego, we place ourselves in a better position to make choices more aligned with our true authentic self, rather than those driven by guilt, fear or inherited beliefs.

In one session, Kay arrived stressed and upset.

"It's him."

"Something happened?" I asked.

"He's left and I think he's seeing someone. I can't be sure, though."

I remained neutral despite the shocking news. Her partner had packed his bags and left. However shocking this sounded, I also acknowledged that Kay had been burying her head in the sand, not wanting to know what he did on the nights he was mysteriously absent.

"You can't be sure?" I asked gently.

"No," Kay answered. "I suspect he may have someone... a mistress. I had my suspicions for a while. I don't know... I just thought it would go away."

Kay looked utterly distressed, betrayed and confused. In that moment, she seemed lost, not just in the relationship, but in herself. She had harboured this suspicion for a while, yet had not brought it into therapy, nor had she confronted him. I knew that Kay suppressed her emotions and didn't disclose all that she needed to, partly because of shame and partly because if she ignored the problem, then it wasn't real and so would magically go away. Something about her domestic situation suited her and distressed her at the same time. It kept her tethered to a known reality, even if it was painful. Whatever the reason, it was perhaps preferable to the disruption and uncertainty that the truth would bring.

"Well, a few days ago, he'd asked me if I could go and stay with my mum for a week. I didn't know what he was planning, but this! I was just thinking he'll get over the affair, but he hasn't. It's all gotten so messy and everyone will find out."

In all that, Kay had revealed that her partner had been having an affair, which she apparently knew about. Sending her to her mother's house meant he could have the freedom to do as he pleased with his mistress, who, it seemed, was in town. It struck me as deeply disrespectful. I raised my brows at this and for once was lost for words.

"I've been okay with him carrying on with this business for one or two nights. I didn't think it was serious. I thought he would come to his senses. Now... well, it's gone way too far."

The revelation presented an opportunity to address what we had been circling for some time–the internal split in Kay's personality. Her rational side tolerated the unacceptable, while her other side buried and enraged, had been silenced. This was an opportunity to direct her rage not inward, not into shame, but outward, and towards a clearer sense of self-respect.

"What do you think?" she asked.

"I'll turn that around," I said gently, "What do *you* think?"

Kay hesitated, her eyes shifting as if weighing the consequences of acknowledging her feelings. Then, with a quiet intensity, she admitted, "I want to kick him out of the house."

"Okay, why don't you?" I asked.

"He owns the house," she said quietly.

Heavy silence.

Finally, Kay looked up and said, "I wish I could take you with me to talk with him."

Kay was more than capable, but this exchange highlighted her lack of belief in her own ability. The situation had eroded her confidence over time, leaving her more reticent than usual.

"You know I can't do that," I replied gently. "But I can see how upsetting this is for you. It feels to me that this isn't what you want, nor what you signed up for. And it's perfectly acceptable to feel that way."

In between sobs, Kay finally reached a decision towards the end of the session. She couldn't cope with the situation and resolved to give him an ultimatum. I was glad to see that she had finally summoned the courage to speak up and not allow him to use her.

She did give her partner an ultimatum: it was either her or the mistress. Surprisingly, he responded with understanding and ended the affair. Once she had acted, Kay began setting boundaries and defining what was acceptable in their relationship. As things didn't fall apart, she gained confidence and started expressing her overall dissatisfaction. She even wondered if she could fully trust her partner or if the relationship was even worth her while. The minimal resistance from her partner and his ready willingness to end the affair felt 'too good to be true', and she sensed something was off.

Kay began organising her life independently. She went out with friends, joined a gym and focused on regaining a sense of autonomy outside of her relationship. The more she did, the more she remembered how much she enjoyed spending time with her friends. Yet, these changes didn't sit well with her partner.

Several sessions later, Kay entered the room looking distraught, her eyes red from crying. She sat down without taking off her coat, as if shielding herself from the world. The coat wasn't just clothing; it was a silent testament to her guardedness, a barrier protecting her from exposure, both physical and emotional.

"If I give up therapy, he'll marry me," she said quietly.

I took a deep breath. "And what do you think about that?"

"It's not what I want to do. But we can also start trying for a child. This is what I want and have always wanted. I knew I would need to compromise."

Her words struck me as odd. The partner's request felt coercive, almost like blackmail. I tried not to judge–they could have their own agreements–but I was concerned about the long-term implications. In his eyes, her therapy was comparable to an affair and posed a threat to his control. Why would her newfound vitality unsettle him? Perhaps because it symbolised her independence and a challenge to the power dynamic that had kept the relationship intact. To him, therapy wasn't a space for healing; it was a rival demanding her time, attention and emotional energy. I could see that Kay had made her choice. She needed to keep up appearances for the families, because anything else was shameful. She feared being seen as the one who couldn't keep a man and therefore seen as a failure. The pressure to keep up appearances wasn't only external; it was internalised. Giving up therapy felt like admitting failure, not just to others, but to herself.

"There are worse things that could happen," Kay added.

"What worse things?" I asked.

"Like not being married."

I wasn't sure Kay realised that I wasn't married. She had probably assumed I was deprived in some way, and her words seemed to reflect that belief. Well, if success was measured in the things we accumulate like a husband, children and possessions, I was lacking a great deal. I wondered how Kay had felt in our first encounter, in the pre-transference before interaction. How much of this stayed with her?

Kay didn't see herself as a Black woman who had made it on their own. Instead, she was defining herself by the shame of separation. The comfort and social acceptance she had come to experience were too much to lose and she could not see herself living any other way.

And true to her word, she didn't return to therapy. Even with my best efforts, I couldn't convince her to continue.

Her desire for a baby was tied into a need for unconditional love. I found it difficult to admit this, but we had succeeded in our work together. Kay got what she wanted in some sense: a baby and a husband and was well on the way to having both.

I have worked with lots of Black women over the years and understand the lengths they go to hide their vulnerabilities while putting up with what is not serving them. However, when given the opportunity to take control of our lives, they would change for the better. As Black women, becoming aware of our strength is as important as knowing where and when we need support. Acceptance of our vulnerability, as well as regaining our agency, is essential in making us whole again. We cannot constantly expect ourselves to do it alone – we can support one another.

Kay's journey demonstrates how therapy is less about solving a problem and more about creating space for self-recognition and agency. Many clients come to therapy with a desire to change, yet fear the very transformation they seek. Change often requires confronting long-standing patterns of behaviour, inherited roles and internalised expectations. For Kay, the split between the competent professional and the subdued partner reflected her history of family hierarchies, gender expectations and internalised beliefs about compromise and self-worth. Therapy offered her a space to articulate her feelings, assert her needs and take steps towards autonomy. Her growth, however incremental, reminds us that people can reclaim power in areas where they previously felt powerless.

The process of therapy is both revealing and corrective; it allows clients to experiment with self-expression, to feel validated and to act in ways aligned with their true selves. Kay's case underscores the delicate balance between support and autonomy, risk and reward, and the courage required to enact meaningful change in life.

Riana: Recovery, Resilience and Belonging

Before starting therapy with me, Riana had been under the care of another therapist. In their work, she had broached the topic of getting to know her Black father. That therapist, who was white and a colleague of mine, then recommended me. In the referral, my colleague shared that they did not feel equipped to support Riana in exploring her Black heritage. Regardless, given that Riana is mixed race, I felt there should have been some room for connection and identification between them.

Even though I knew my colleague was trying to be helpful, I could not help but wonder how their recommendation would be interpreted by Riana. Could she have experienced the referral as a continuation of the work, or as a rejection of her Black side? I carried this question into our first session, knowing that the way she had been passed on to me might have already directed the course of our interaction.

Despite this uncertainty, I was mindful of how much hope was being invested in me by both Riana and my colleague. I knew I had to tread carefully and not to inadvertently compound her shame–the shame of feeling disconnected from her Black heritage, of being partially unseen or of struggling to claim a part of herself that society and even therapists might not fully acknowledge.

Riana began telling her life story in detail which I could tell she had rehearsed. This is not uncommon: some clients arrive with a prepared monologue, while others seek more direction. Either way, the first encounter often sets the tone.

Her narrative came out in a rushed manner, in fact, like pulling off a plaster. She appeared to want to get it all out; otherwise, she may not have been able to finish. There was clear determination in her telling, though it also felt tinged with desperation. I stayed attentive as she spoke. As she ran out of breath, I sensed she was becoming overwhelmed. She stopped briefly and looked at me nervously. I waited patiently. I knew this therapeutic outlet was important to her–a space where what needed to be said could finally be spoken.

"We've got time," I commented gently.

Riana managed to get through the monologue. As she reached the end, her shoulders dropped noticeably and she exhaled a long, shaky breath, as though she had been holding it in the entire time. Her hands, clenched in her lap, slowly relaxed. It seemed she had fully unburdened herself. This took a great deal of courage.

"I don't know if any of that made sense," she said quietly. "I've never said it all out loud before." She then paused before continuing. "My family don't show their emotions. It feels difficult to bear at times. But my mother recently announced over lunch that the man I had always believed was my father is not my father."

A thick, heavy pause filled the room.

"How terribly painful that must have been," I said softly.

"We were fighting," Riana continued. "I don't even remember what it was about, but my mother just let it out. It was like the ground shifted under me. One moment I was eating lunch, and the next, I didn't know who I was."

She glanced up, her eyes brimming with tears, held back with effort. "And no one talked about it again. It was like she dropped a bomb and then went back to her sandwich."

Her mother had kept this secret for many years. She explained that Riana's biological father was someone she knew and had an affair with; that affair led to her pregnancy with Riana. The disclosure was delivered as a matter of fact, with little apparent concern for how it might land. Riana described, through sobs, the horror of hearing this revelation. Later, fragments of her life began to make sense. I felt deep sympathy for the betrayal of trust she had endured.

"My biological father was married. And get this… to a friend of my mother's. My family wants to keep it all a secret because it would expose the affair and bring shame on the family."

It seemed the truth had been revealed in anger, and now Riana was expected to carry the secret herself, bearing both shame and pain. As she spoke, it occurred to me that this was the first time she had been given the space to let it all out.

I found myself disapproving of the way her mother had disclosed this information. The feeling rose swiftly with a tightening in my chest, and a flash of protective anger on Riana's behalf. Why reveal such a painful truth in this way, knowing the harm it could cause? Her mother had carried the pain for years, only to release it vindictively during a heated moment, transferring the burden onto Riana. I had to sit with this disapproval carefully. In the room, I could not afford to align too closely with Riana's experience of her mother as cruel, even though her account suggested real cruelty. To do so might foreclose her ability to hold the complexity of the fact that her mother was both victim and perpetrator, both wounded and wounding. Instead, I focused on bearing witness to Riana's pain, allowing her to feel the full weight of what had been done to her, without rushing to judgment or rescue.

This secret had been revealed during an Easter visit to her mother's home in Zanzibar, where the family lived. After returning to the UK, Riana had 3 months to reflect and process before she started therapy with me. She began to re-examine her childhood memories. Growing up, she recalled overhearing heated conversations between her parents that would abruptly stop when she entered the room. She sensed they were about her but never knew why. This left her feeling like a problem.

"I felt detached from the family," she said. "But I was always provided for. I went to good schools and they paid for me to travel. But what I needed was to believe that I was loved."

I wondered whether her mother's investment in education was also an attempt to counteract shame by shaping Riana into someone worthy of pride. Perhaps if Riana could be exceptional, the mother could justify her existence and redeem the affair that produced her.

Shame is a deeply painful emotion, often associated with powerlessness. Over time, it can erode self-worth and instil a fear of being seen. When Riana's mother became pregnant, she'd hoped Riana's father would choose her. His rejection likely generated profound shame, which Riana had to endure through what was said and not said as well as her mother's actions. However, mixed in with the distress was relief because Riana realised she was not the problem; the problem belonged to her mother.

Riana was of mixed heritage, born to a white mother and a Black biological father she had not known. Her mother had married a white man when Riana was very young, and he was the only father she had ever known. Together they had another daughter, who was white. Riana felt her sister was treated much better than she had been. She did need more care and attention, and Riana rationalised this difference by telling herself it was natural. But the reality was sharper than that: she was the only mixed race person in an otherwise white household, and her darker skin set her apart in ways no one openly acknowledged. In addition, Riana took part in caring for her young sibling and the man she thought was her father. Their relationship had always been a distant one, but she assumed that was just the way he was. As attention was focused on the younger child, Riana became vulnerable. She disclosed being molested as a teenager by a handyman – something she had never told anyone. Speaking out would have risked exposure and further shame.

"Perhaps you kept quiet about the abuse because it would have been made to be your problem. As a result, you kept quiet to keep safe. It was the only way, as a child, you could protect yourself from a cruel and indifferent adult world."

"Exactly," Riana responded sombrely.

The session ended in silence – the kind that follows when a harsh truth is finally spoken.

Over the following weeks, we returned to this abuse several times. Riana's silence around it had not only been strategic – it had become a template for how she managed all potentially shameful information about herself. The abuse had confirmed what she already suspected: that her needs did not matter, that speaking up would only make things worse, and that she was fundamentally alone. In our work together, we began to slowly dismantle this belief, creating a space where speaking was not only safe but transformative.

Riana had other reasons to feel different. Apart from being mixed race, she had few common features with the rest of her family. At one point, her sister had asked her if she was adopted, causing a further awareness of how different she looked from everyone else. Riana soon internalised shame about her appearance and this was compounded by her observation that lighter-skinned family members were treated more favourably. Her mother also carried shame, not only about the affair, but also about having slept with a Black man, even though she had wanted a relationship with him. Riana and her darker skin served as a constant reminder of what she, her mother, had done. To Riana all these shades of shame were a painful rejection of who she was.

Psychologists Kenneth and Mamie Clark carried out an experiment between 1939 and 1940 where children were given dolls of different ethnic groups to play with. Both Black and white children were asked which doll they liked. Each group gave positive attributes to white dolls and negative attributes to Black dolls. When asked which doll was nice, which was pretty, which they would like to play with, children of both races consistently chose the white doll. When asked which doll looked bad or which they did not like, they pointed to the Black doll. Crucially, when Black children were asked which doll looked most like them, many pointed to the Black doll and then fell silent or showed visible distress. The experiment revealed that by early childhood, Black children had already absorbed society's racial hierarchy and turned it inward against themselves.This result shouldn't be surprising, as built into language is a particular order and hierarchy of the world: the way we use words defines what is good and bad. Language has been used to adversely affect Black people making us a symbolic representation of all that is dark and ugly. Black children, once they become better able to extrapolate information they acquire from the world, become more sensitive about skin colour.

When Frantz Fanon stated in *Black Skin, White Masks* that, 'I know nothing about black women,' he was referring to how Black women are not seen as desired in the same way as white women who have been embellished as feminine in western traditions. The lack of desire for Black women is not because they are unattractive but since beauty and femininity are not normally apportioned to them. It is a social construct where those attributes are apportioned to fair-skinned women. As a result, Black women are rendered seemingly genderless. No wonder Riana believed skin colour was a problem. In understanding this, I have found the writings of Black feminist authors to be helpful. The work of bell hooks, Audre Lorde and Toni Morrison, for example, have brought to light the oppression of Black women and continually redefined and empowered them.

I thought Riana had a beautiful skin tone though I did not communicate this verbally in our early sessions. Doing so might have felt hollow and come across as just another voice telling her how she should see herself. Instead, I tried to convey through my presence and the steadiness of my attention, that I saw her fully and without judgment. As therapists, we try to communicate a loving acceptance of our client. We become the mirror, not one that is impermeable but one where the self is reflected and validated. Despite this, I wondered whether my silence around her appearance might also have been a repetition of the family pattern – another person failing to name what was so painfully obvious to her. In later sessions, when our rapport had deepened, I found moments to reflect what I genuinely saw: her strength, her resilience and her beauty. These were not platitudes, but observations grounded in the work we had done together.

Our loving acceptance as therapists is conveyed through the work. This is why it takes time, through continuity and sameness, to bear and offer what is digestible at a given time. I believe the work for reparation lies here, where the client feels seen, which describes a state in which the therapist fully recognises the client's multiplicity.

Riana worked long hours as a restaurant manager and struggled with isolation. She feared that closeness would expose her past.

"At home, I mostly connect online," she said. "Even then, I'm careful. I'm anxious all the time. It's lonely."

"What feels most frightening about people finding out?" I asked.

"I'm not sure. It's been a long-kept secret and the way I keep it is not to talk about myself much," she replied.

"I get it," I said.

She paused. "It means I feel unsure about everything. I can't quite say why," she continued. "I wonder whether it's because no one is allowed to know me fully... I do like my job, though. It distracts me."

I sensed she was stuck between past and future, unable to inhabit the present fully. The secrecy had become both protection and prison. Slowly, over many months, she began discovering what brought pleasure – bingo nights, the little things, the ritual of our weekly sessions where she could tell me stories about her week without fear of exposure.

Christopher Bollas' *Being a Character*, suggests that psychoanalysis often focuses narrowly on symptoms that have caused expressed mental suffering (1992). Working through past trauma represents an important part of the work, yet there may be an over-emphasis on what is not working as opposed to what is.

I found myself mindful of this tendency as I worked with Riana, and in my work with Black women more generally. It would have been easy to focus exclusively on her wounds:

the paternity revelation, the sexual abuse, the internalized racism, and in doing so miss the ways she had already been surviving, adapting and building a life. At times, the analytic focus on trauma can become exhaustive, risking a foreclosure of the subject's existing capacities. Straddling vulnerability and resilience often functions as a strategic psychic position: a way of remaining open to suffering without being reduced to it, and of asserting agency without disavowing injury.

We should acknowledge the past can influence the future. Nonetheless, the past does not have to determine the future. In this way, we work towards breaking the cycle of trauma-based habits derived as a defence against further pain. Psychoanalysis, I believe, is not overly in favour of celebrating clients' achievements, but given the lack of attuned others in their lives, this form of nurturing and acceptance can be transformative.

For example, during our work together, Riana was promoted to a supervisory role. This gave her confidence and greater freedom. She could now do things she had not thought of doing previously. I was genuinely delighted and praised her achievement, not as a therapeutic strategy but from a place of authentic pride in her growth.

She arrived at one session visibly lighter. "I told my manager about some of my ideas," she said. "She actually listened."

"That's wonderful," I said. "What was it like to be heard?"

"Strange," she admitted. "I kept waiting for her to dismiss me. But she didn't."

This moment marked a shift. Riana was beginning to expect something different from the world that was not rejection or indifference, but recognition.

Perhaps I came to symbolise the accepting father she barely knew. My acceptance gave her newfound confidence and curiosity. Over time, Riana began to believe that she could try to have a relationship with her biological father. This could potentially become a new source of love and acceptance she had been looking for.

The process of reaching this decision was gradual and fraught. Some weeks she came to the sessions determined to make contact; other weeks she would retreat, convinced that he would reject her just as her mother's shame had rejected her. I did not push. Instead, I held the possibility open, allowing her to move towards it at her own pace.

"What if he doesn't want to know me?" she asked one afternoon.

"That would be painful," I acknowledged. "But it would also tell you something important–that his limitations are not about your worth."

She sat with this for a long moment.

"I think I need to try," she said finally. "Even if he says no, at least I'll know. I won't spend the rest of my life wondering."

As the weeks went by, Riana arrived at this conclusion more firmly. If the biological father couldn't accept her and they couldn't have a relationship, she was comfortable enough in therapy that she would inevitably be okay. She had begun to build an internal sense of worth that was not contingent on his approval.

"At the very least," she said, "I've got you."

I felt the weight of that statement–both the gift and the responsibility. She had invested in me the hope that someone could see her fully and not turn away. In that moment, I hoped I had lived up to it.

What began as a search for her father became a journey towards healing, self-knowledge and confidence in being. Riana was learning to inhabit herself more fully, to claim the parts of her identity that had been sources of shame and to imagine a future where she was not defined solely by what had been done to her. The work was far from finished, but something essential had shifted: she no longer believed she had to carry her secrets alone.

Working with Riana required me to hold several tensions at once. I had to be mindful of the referral itself–passed from a white therapist who felt inadequately equipped–and what this might have signalled to her about her Blackness being a problem requiring specialist intervention. My strongest countertransference came in response to her mother's casual cruelty. I felt protective anger, which I had to manage carefully so as not to make the mother the 'bad cop' and position myself as the rescuing 'good parent.' Riana needed space to hold the complexity–that her mother was both wounded and wounding.

I made a deliberate choice to step away from traditional therapeutic restraint. When Riana was promoted, I celebrated with her genuinely. Given her history of being told she was unwanted, maintaining professional distance risked repeating the very indifference that had harmed her. She needed to be seen and valued, not just analysed.

The work reminded me that therapy with clients who have been systematically devalued requires more than technical skill. It requires a willingness to be changed by the encounter, to celebrate their growth and to sit with the uncertainty of not knowing how their story ends.

Yvette: Money, Agency and Power

Yvette was measuredly articulate over the telephone. Her accent was polished, confident and self-assured making me associate her with private schools, red brick universities and the like. She wanted help navigating issues in life, particularly around work. Yvette had a clear idea of what was needed. She spoke with clarity about what she thought was wrong and what needed to change. But I found myself wondering how receptive she would be to psychotherapy–whether she was seeking deeper exploration or hoping for quick, solution-focused advice.

I discovered, to my surprise at our first meeting, that Yvette was a Black woman. I questioned why being Black shouldn't sound like Yvette and was clearly responding to a wider stereotype. I wondered whether she had experienced people making assumptions about her ahead of meeting face-to-face.

The name was what had thrown me. Yvette had an English-sounding surname. Of course, there is a historical basis for this which is that many Black people inherited the surnames of their slave owners. Even today, the expectation still carries that English-sounding names are generally associated with white people.

We are often told that we live in a meritocracy, yet research shows otherwise. Studies have found that job applicants with names perceived as 'foreign' or non-Anglicised are significantly less likely to be invited for interviews. One UK study, for example, found that applicants with names associated with ethnic minorities had to send out 60% more CVs to get the same number of call-backs as those with traditionally English names. Di Stasio (2019). I have had Black clients with English-sounding names tell of the surprised look from interviewers when they walked through the door.

Yvette was well presented. Her hair was set in a neat pony tail. She wore a loose tweed skirt and a flowery top. While in her mid-30s, Yvette looked older than her years. She seemed conservative in appearance but also under some strain. When she walked in, she immediately explained that she had hip pain which prevented her from sitting for too long.

"Please, stand if you need to," I responded.

After thanking me, she launched into her life story. Well, less her life story, more a CV. Yvette rattled through qualifications and achievements. Moreover, she gave a summary of the courses she'd taken. Yvette was rightly proud of her accomplishments. There was a wish to impress, too. I sensed that it was important to Yvette to see that I was aware of her intellectual capabilities.

I was accordingly impressed and reflected on how people may feel intimidated by her and how, perhaps, that was the objective. Occasionally, as we've seen in Kay's story, when someone presents an overtly confident front, it can be a cover-up for some other problem.

"So, I've come to you because I want help with moving up the career ladder," Yvette said. "I may have to do some more training. Yes I've managed to do a lot. I know as people tell me but I'm not where I want to be yet. Something is holding me back. I'm not quite sure what, and it's making me feel very depressed."

"Sounds like you've invested much in your career and accomplished a lot already," I responded. "You've just been telling me that."

"Yes, but it's not enough."

I waited for her to say more. My silence was to give her space for more self-reflection. It is often the case that the client expects to be given the answers. However, an attentive presence can get them to provide their own thoughts on a matter, offering intervention when necessary. Yvette sat quietly for a while. Her eyes drifted to the floor, then to the window. One hand fidgeted with the strap of her bag. Her shoulders were hunched and her expression was drawn–contemplative, but uncertain, perhaps even uneasy. After a quiet minute, she resumed.

Eventually, I realised that her career was not what needed fixing. Perhaps this striving for career success had come due to a lack in her personal life. Yvette needed a certain stillness to catch up with where she was. Given the inequalities in areas of employment, many people find themselves preoccupied with survival, often at the expense of other areas of life. Yvette was no exception.

The next few meetings proceeded in this way. Yvette was mainly dedicated to work. She had made significant progress, having been promoted several times. She had been exceptionally motivated, and she made sure that all the necessary training courses were taken.

She described herself as being 'a problem solver'. She was the colleague that others came to for help and support. As an inspector, Yvette had a thorough understanding of how the transport department functioned. But it was also because she was always ready to get stuck into the problems other people brought to her. That reliability, however, often left her feeling taken for granted and rarely feeling supported herself. This position left her feeling frustrated, drained and resentful.

This frustration was also palpable in our work. My initial worries about Yvette had been confirmed: she struggled with the ambiguity of not-knowing because she wanted immediate results, and in addition to that, she struggled with the process of getting them. Therapy was highlighting not only her frustration but also her deep unease with vulnerability.

The idea that progress might come from staying with uncertainty–rather than rushing to resolve it–felt alien to Yvette. But she was probably not alone in this. Many clients initially find the process disorienting. It can feel messy and uncomfortable at first, especially for those used to being in control.

Yvette found herself getting angrier as we progressed. The work required time to deliberately reflect, which was alien to her. She was very much used to commanding the show, keeping everything moving and never really thinking much about feelings.

"These feelings you're having are not unusual," I clarified for her. "You're very much in touch with what needs doing to make things work. Here, we have a different focus. We are going to talk about you and your desires for life."

Yvette appeared calmer for a minute.

I returned to asking whether she had pursued her career so aggressively as a way of avoiding other aspects of her life. After all, there was little else she had touched on outside of work and accomplishments.

"What do you want besides that professional growth?" I asked.

Yvette paused. Her eyes dropping for a moment, she looked embarrassed. "A family," she responded quietly.

"A family," I repeated.

For the first time, the focus was widened or redirected, shifting beyond career ambitions to encompass her deeper, more personal desires. Yvette again broke eye contact.

"Yes, a family. I hate being single. I think about having a family all the time."

It was a significant confession, one that exposed her vulnerability and suggested she was beginning to relax, perhaps even trust the therapeutic process. It had taken a long time to share this line of thinking. She seemingly felt as though this was a shameful confession, both of wanting a family and not having achieved it. I realised this was the actual wish, not a desire to advance the career.

Yvette didn't feel there was anyone she could talk with about her loneliness. She had not shared her private wishes with anyone outside of therapy. When her family tried to broach the subject, she would lie about seeing someone. Unlike work, here was an area where she felt she had failed, where achieving her goal felt impossible.

I wondered aloud, "What about friends? Do you have people you can open up to about how you're feeling?"

Yvette shook her head slowly. "No, not really. I'm careful about what I share. It's easier to keep this part of me to myself." She paused before continuing. "I haven't met any men who like me or want to be with me for my personality. I have given up on online dating. It just doesn't work. There are so few decent men out there. And the few that exist, they are all married." Yvette ended with a sigh.

I had heard similar complaints from plenty of single clients, both men and women. While that pain is the same, each person's struggle in their search for love needs to be treated on an individual basis. Yvette, with her current lifestyle, hardly made time for socialising. However, she seemed to me to have so much going for her. She was ambitious, bright, helpful and attractive. I felt there was something crucial missing in the way she had framed her problem.

This is a common trend I've noticed in how people talk about their challenges. Often, the narratives we construct can limit our view. One is focusing on what's absent or what's 'wrong', rather than recognising strengths, opportunities or alternative perspectives. It's in this reframing that new possibilities can emerge. Who were these men who didn't like her? Was the problem really that men didn't like her? Or had she simply not yet met the right person who shared her values? Yvette had said she wanted a family, but what she really wanted was to be seen and recognised. I believed family would come one way or another.

"What kind of partner are you looking for?" I asked her. "What qualities would they possess?"

She told me she preferred white men but often did not get picked, especially on dating sites. She believed that Black men were less dependable and that most preferred white women. Yvette's beliefs reflected broader social trends in racial preferences in online dating, where Black women and Asian men receive fewer responses, shaped by deep-rooted societal stereotypes. As bell hooks argued in *Ain't I a Woman* (1981), Black women have historically been denied the markers of femininity afforded to white women and rendered outside the boundaries of desirability as a consequence of race rather than anything intrinsic to them. This exclusion has deep roots. When Sojourner Truth addressed the Women's Rights Convention in Akron, Ohio in 1851, her rhetorical question, 'Ain't I a woman?', exposed precisely this contradiction: that the category of 'woman,' with all its attendant protections and idealisation, was in practice a racialised category from which Black women were systematically excluded. hooks' title is a deliberate echo of that challenge, locating her 1981 analysis within a tradition of Black feminist resistance stretching back more than a century. The desexualisation of Asian men in western culture follows a parallel logic, rooted in racialised representations that strip away masculinity and sexual agency

But beyond this preference, which I felt reflected a stereotypical view rather than one informed by personal experience, Yvette found it difficult to talk about what she wanted and needed from a potential partner. This made sense, given the wider context of her life. As the only person in her extended family to have achieved what is considered 'success', she was viewed as capable, regularly called for and doted upon, celebrated and even idolised. Within this image of strength, there was little room for vulnerability. Expressing her desires, particularly emotional or relational ones, risked disrupting that narrative.

Yvette was the one everybody in her family–her siblings her nieces and nephews–went to. Everybody visited her during the holidays when the parents were unavailable. She catered for them, preparing food with all the trimmings and bought all the presents. Yvette was essentially the substitute mum because her mother was 'easily overwhelmed' and quite frail physically because of arthritis. She also spoke about how she felt responsible for her mother, worrying that without additional support, apart from her father, she wouldn't be able to cope. Yvette's own needs were being hindered while supporting her parents, but she felt guilty about abandoning them.

"I disappear off somewhere remote when the stress gets too much," Yvette said. "Newcastle or way up north. Places where no one knows me."

"Sounds like when things get overwhelming, you can't find solace in those around you. You need to escape for that."

Given her family dynamics and the pressure of her professional life, Yvette didn't have much time to form relationships. She became progressively disillusioned. While Caucasian men found her physically attractive, they rarely expressed interest in anything long-term. Her experience was that she was often sexualised or fetishised, reduced to stereotypes of Black women as 'exotic' or 'hypersexual.' These encounters left her feeling objectified rather than seen. With her most recent experience, Yvette had held on to a cherished friendship, hoping it would develop further, but was disappointed when she found out that he only wanted a platonic relationship.

Ultimately, despite her achievements, generosity and loyalty, she struggled to see herself as someone others would truly choose. Yvette simply felt undesirable. She came to this conclusion with no awareness of how much she had moulded herself to fit in by adapting her behaviour, hiding parts of herself and softening her presence. All this she had done to be accepted, to become what she thought others wanted, but at the expense of who she truly was.

As we progressed, Yvette grappled with how to be visible, not just professionally or romantically, but as a whole person. It was both symbolic and a practical shift. She began a makeover process, changing her hair from its long, straight cut to a bob. At the same time, she began wearing more subtle colours. She wanted to look metropolitan.

"Trying to move away from grey clothing," she explained. Her aim was to choose what reflected her true self.

Over time, I witnessed Yvette relaxing further into the work. She spoke about earlier experiences, including her time at college. She was often the only Black person in the class. Being the only Black face was something she became used to and rarely questioned. Throughout her college years, Yvette felt accepted for her grades, politeness and the way she presented herself. Unpacking these memories, Yvette began to see how much she had internalised the idea that acceptance came through adaptation, not authenticity.

For her, anti-black racism was not a topic her family spoke about. They just got on with things. Any talk of this kind was met with irritation with the rationale steeped in resignation as part of the collective attitude in her home.

"What can we do about it?" was always the closing question.

She had trained herself never to pay any attention to that aspect of her identity.

Yvette did not feel she experienced any difficulties related to race at college, despite being one of the few Black students there. Instead, she navigated other challenges: the pressure of maintaining top grades, balancing part-time work alongside studies and fitting into social circles that felt unfamiliar or exclusive. She sometimes felt isolated during group projects, unsure of how to assert herself without being judged, and struggled with homesickness and the emotional weight of being far from family. While she was aware of occasional derogatory remarks, she laughed them off. Denial became a coping mechanism, a defence strategy she employed both consciously and subconsciously to navigate situations where she felt exposed or vulnerable.

The split–a separation between her own success and the reality of structural inequality, was clear in Yvette's view of how other Black women were treated at work. Fully acknowledging systemic racism might have threatened the personal story she relied on: that effort and competence alone determined outcomes. She noticed that Black women often missed out on promotions, yet she herself had little direct experience of racism. The split acted as a protective mechanism, letting her maintain confidence and a sense of control. Diversity initiatives existed, but she never felt the need to attend; her hard work had shielded her from the microaggression others faced. I was surprised to hear that she wasn't fazed by this. After all, she could see that people who looked like her were being discriminated against. Any form of identification with them seemed non-existent.

Black Talent Charter in collaboration with Bain & Company (2024) highlighted that in financial and other professional services, Black employees represent less than 1% of senior leadership roles, despite comprising 4.4% of the working-age population and 13.5% of London's population. To climb that ladder, many people of colour have had to mould themselves consciously or unconsciously into something closer to the Caucasian norm – the cultural behaviours, values, diction, beauty standards and social expectations typical or dominant within white communities.

In predominantly white environments, there is significant pressure for people of colour to adapt or conform to these norms in order to fit in, be accepted, or advance professionally. However, when people of colour express this desire for acceptance or make moves to be accepted, they are often rejected. Although Britain is considered home to many Black British people, even that categorisation of "Black British" locates them not just as British but insists on their otherness.

Yvette was aware of the negative portrayal of Black people by society. But she didn't see herself as Black, or at least, not in the same way as 'them'–those others–and therefore anti-black racism, in her view, did not happen to her.

For some people, there may be a real powerlessness in thinking and talking about race and racism; discussing it can feel like a way of keeping the topic alive. As a result, silence becomes a form of distancing, making racism seem like something that happens to other people. Ignoring it then becomes easier. This is not a privilege most Black people have, as they are often on the receiving end of negative projections and lived experiences. White people, in contrast, can go their entire lives without having to think about race until confronted with it, often through the presence of a Black person. But whether spoken about or not, it is a reality and a structural and social one. Racism, like sexism and other forms of hatred of difference, exists.

Yvette had not explicitly mentioned race as a problem but had picked a Black therapist. By unconsciously doing so, I inferred that the intimate realities of race were an aspect of her therapy that she had not known how to talk about until we began our work. There are intersecting aspects of any client's narrative which get explored concurrently. Being Black is only one aspect of a client's identity. The exploration that takes place in the therapeutic setting is how this aspect is integral to their existence. The same goes for other markers of social identity such as sexuality or gender; for some, they are all occurring simultaneously.

Personal disclosure on aspects of racism requires something more than just empathy. The client needs to know the therapist is on board. Being on board means showing signs that the therapist understands the lived experience of racism–not just in theory, but as a force that shapes daily living. It's not enough to feel that their therapist is kind or well-meaning; they need to know the therapist is with them.

When entering emotionally risky or painful terrain, like Yvette, clients need to feel confident that the person sitting opposite them understands the stakes and won't retreat, minimise or shift away from the discomfort. And this is not simply won by virtue of being Black. Yes, it helps, but it doesn't mean we necessarily share the same values or valuations of the same topic.

With any form of oppression, something of a togetherness needs to be spelt out; otherwise, the client can be left feeling this is their problem alone. Effective psychotherapy needs to consider multiple identities moving in and out of the cultural realm but at the same time embracing it. A single self can have many identities–racial, gendered, sexual, cultural and more, sometimes in harmony, sometimes in tension. Ultimately, identity is always defined on one's own terms.

This approach aligns closely with Kimberlé Crenshaw's concept of intersectionality, which emphasises how overlapping systems of oppression such as racism, sexism, classism and heteronormativity interact to shape lived experience (Crenshaw, 1991). Thus, in psychotherapy, the task is not to resolve the multiplicity of identities into a singular narrative, but to create space where these identities can coexist, be explored and be validated. It is through this process that individuals can begin to articulate their own meaning, on their own terms.

Yvette feared ending up alone despite her evident success. She was deeply dissatisfied and spent endless hours sitting at home, rarely going out and finding little joy in her day-to-day life. Her professional achievements felt hollow without a sense of personal fulfilment. Though Yvette had worked so hard to set up a reputable career, she felt as though this wasn't enough.

She knew that something had to change, but she didn't know what or how to do it. Throughout her whole life, both with family and work, she had never rocked the boat. Like Leah, whose story we explored earlier, Yvette had always sought to please others. For Yvette, toeing the line meant that she could be seen as the person that everybody else came to; even though this meant succeeding on other people's terms, she had survived, and on the surface, it looked as though she was thriving.

After many sessions together, it was becoming apparent that Yvette was beginning to allow herself to explore who she might become, not by declaring what she wanted, but by giving space for previously unspoken desires and conflicts to emerge within the safety of the therapeutic relationship. She began to give herself permission to lean into the therapy, and was relieved to have the opportunity to focus on herself. Gradually, she valued the space. Once the dam was opened, a torrent was released. Our sessions uncovered so many things that she wanted to do but had not been able to see a way to do. I tried nurturing a sense of internal permission and curiosity in her, holding the space where she could begin to imagine, perhaps for the first time, what a life shaped more on her terms might feel like.

One result of this was that Yvette started self-defence classes with some of her colleagues. She was keen to get stronger and fitter, and it was also a good way of making new friends. Gaining an awareness of herself and getting a tighter grasp of her needs started to make her feel more empowered to bring about change. The general niggling that something wasn't quite right, which she had assumed had something to do with not getting promoted, was seen for what it really was: a need to live a life that felt more expansive and filled with her own choices.

"I worry that if I don't work as hard as I do, people will think that I'm not good enough," Yvette admitted with a pained expression. Her usually rigid posture seemed to sag. I was also mindful that she was in a predominantly male environment.

"Good enough for who, I wonder?" I questioned.

Yvette chuckled; she saw the point. She was near the top in her chosen field but had forgotten how to dream and make plans. Instead she focused on who she was at work and what she represented to colleagues. In spaces dominated by men, being a woman, especially a Black woman, often means having to prove yourself twice over. Even if race wasn't what she consciously named, the demands of gendered expectations in that space may have shaped her more than she realised. Yvette didn't need a promotion for the obvious reasons of security and success. She needed a promotion to master a situation as a promotion as a symbolic victory, proving through status that she belonged. Yvette realised that she needed to set her own goals and define herself for herself; otherwise, she would continuously be managed by the expectations of others.

When she developed an injury in self-defence class her hip pain was aggravated. Going to work became difficult. Yvette finally consulted a specialist, who suggested that she might need hip replacement surgery. This was a wake-up call.

Initially, she was afraid to take time off work as in her mind, it would impact any opportunity for progression. However, given the gravity of the situation, she was able to work up the courage to ask for medical leave. In the end, the operation went ahead without any complications. During her leave, Yvette realised that she had needed and wanted to take time off for years.

During this period, I discovered that Yvette owned a telescope, something never mentioned before. She used it for birdwatching. Her garden was spacious and attracted a variety of birds. These restful moments provided space for physical and emotional recuperation. By the time she regained full health, Yvette firmly believed the birds had saved her life.

Life continued with help from the birds; they reminded Yvette to stay present and enjoy the life around her without expectation or reward. She was surprised to find that her life or sense of self hadn't fallen apart outside of work. The time away affirmed that she could exist outside of productivity. She began to rediscover who she was when she wasn't being evaluated, promoted or relied upon. Stillness meant healing. She was an important, well-respected and highly-regarded member of her team. In addition, she had allies and colleagues were genuinely concerned about her wellbeing.

When she returned to work, at first, she tried to return as the 'old Yvette,' but the internal shift had been significant. She now saw her work environment through a different lens. Microaggression, unequal pay and long-ignored biases now stood out starkly. She became frustrated and angry. As she tackled this frustration, she also decided to work on prioritising herself and doing more outside of work. She talked about travel, more as a way of breaking out of the commitments found within family and work.

"Maybe somewhere even further than Newcastle," Yvette laughed.

Just over a year into her recovery and return to work, Yvette was invited to take over an important task force. On paper, it was everything she had worked towards for years; the long-awaited promotion had arrived. But instead of excitement, she felt a knot of unease. The opportunity was prestigious, but it demanded a commitment that would tether her to responsibilities, thus consuming her freedom, interrupting plans she had for travel and limiting the space she had fought to carve out for herself. The instinct to accept the opportunity was strong, shaped by years of believing that success was synonymous with worth. Yet something had shifted. This time, she didn't immediately say yes.

She found herself caught between old habits and new values after having tasted a different rhythm of life. She now had an identity beyond her professional role. Taking on the task force would mean shelving those things, at least for some time. Part of her still wanted to follow the old script–accept, achieve prove herself–but another part recognised the importance of staying true to her own needs and pace. She lingered in that tension, weighing ambition against autonomy and obligation against self-care.

After much thought, Yvette deferred taking on the role. It wasn't a rejection of ambition, but a deliberate choice to honour what she now understood about herself. Growth isn't only measured by promotions, but also by the ability to listen inwardly and say no when the cost feels too high. I was happy for Yvette. She had taken charge and been able to prioritise herself rather than accept what other people expected of her.

Yvette's story reminded me that success and capability do not automatically bring fulfilment. She had spent so long moulding herself to meet the expectations of work, family and society that she had almost forgotten what it meant to want something for herself. The little things, like taking a moment to stop, birdwatching and taking care of her own needs, were as transformative as any promotion or achievement. Change didn't happen in a single step; it came in giving herself permission to be seen, to pause and to define her own life. In doing so, Yvette began to discover that the life she wanted wasn't somewhere out of reach – it had been waiting for her attention all along.

Amie: Identity, Culture and Connection

Money is like sex; when the topic comes up, people either get uncomfortable or excited. Both subjects are often tied to deep-seated beliefs, desires and fears. While psychoanalysis is excellent for talking about sex, helping us unpack shame, desire and identity, when it comes to money, it falls short. Talking about money can evoke discomfort, guilt, envy, pride or secrecy. We may feel judged for having too much, too little or for wanting more. Where sex is often explored in therapeutic settings, money remains the taboo of all taboos.

During my psychotherapy training, the 'business' of being a therapist wasn't really covered. That's because a therapist, like an artist, charges what they feel their work is worth. But how do you put a price on such a service? The act of doing so is fraught. Charge too much, and it may imply an overpromise of what can be delivered. Charge too little, and the work can be minimised or even undervalued. But there is also the question of how much clients can afford. If prices are set too high, you exclude people who could really benefit from therapy but cannot readily afford it.

The fee constitutes part of the therapeutic frame, just as time and place do. Time – same day, same hour each week – provides predictability and safety, allowing clients to feel held within a stable container. Sessions begin and end on time, reinforcing a sense of reliability and mutual respect. The place, whether a physical office or a virtual space, serves as a psychological holding environment, separate from the chaos of daily life. The fee sets boundaries around value. It is paid in exchange for the therapist's time, expertise and engagement. But a therapist cannot guarantee health or recovery. Likewise, paying more does not guarantee a 'cure.'

As therapists, we hope to provide unconditional care towards our clients in an environment where healing, repair and potentially growth can take place. We aim to create a space for awareness, possibilities, truth and change. In some ways, this resembles the idealised relationship a parent has with a child. But parents don't charge by the hour. By doing so, the therapist introduces a limit to the love: for 50 to 60 minutes a week, or bi-monthly, and for a fee, there is unconditional care. Outside of that, conditions apply.

In therapy, I have had clients who want to negotiate fees; Amie was one of them. This comes down to several interwoven factors. Some clients grew up in countries where bartering is the norm, so negotiating with a therapist might be normal. It may also be partly due to socio-economic factors. On average, Black people earn less than white people, reflecting a racial pay gap. According to the UK's Office for National Statistics, the median hourly pay for Black employees is significantly lower than for white employees (ONS, 2023). In 2022, Black full-time employees earned approximately 5.6% less per hour than their white counterparts.

Beyond socio-economic inequalities, there is often scepticism or distrust about what therapy can offer Black people. Central to all of this is the idea of value: what society assigns to us and, consequently, what value we assign to ourselves. This is rooted in the historic and systemic undervaluing of Black people. It is no coincidence, then, that people of colour frequently have to fight to assert their worth. This internalised devaluation occurs not only between Black and white relationships but also within Black communities themselves. Power dynamics that play out in the therapeutic setting mirror broader social dynamics, including those between Black therapists and Black clients. In some cases, clients struggle to assign value to their therapist, reflecting internalised tensions around worth and recognition.

When Amie, a Black British woman in her late 30s, sought therapy, she came as a dietician working two days a week at a GP practice and freelancing alongside that. She lived with her partner and their three-year-old son. During our assessment, the first thing Amie told me was that money might be a problem. She could only afford to pay a certain amount, which turned out to be significantly less than my fee. Now, my fee was neither extortionate nor the lowest in my area. I felt that my charges were reasonable without making therapy virtually inaccessible for most people. Nevertheless, when Amie said she couldn't pay my full fee, I asked what she could afford. She offered a lower amount, and I accepted. Perhaps things would have gone differently if I hadn't. Perhaps I had already set the tone that the cost, value and contract of my services were open to negotiation.

I have long been committed to encouraging greater diversity, not only among clients but also in training and the profession more broadly. I try to support people who want to work with me, particularly those from marginalised backgrounds who may face structural barriers to accessing training, mentorship and professional development. In this sense, my decision was informed by a rationale like that used by some training institutions, which offer bursaries or reduced fees in recognition of unequal access to financial and educational resources.

Many people decide to become practitioners following positive experiences as clients, and where possible, I support that progression. Sometimes I accept a lower fee to make therapy accessible to those who may later train in the field themselves. Training to become a therapist carries significant financial costs and those costs are not borne equally. In an ideal and equitable system, professional value and fees would not need to be negotiated in this way. But access to both healthcare and professional training remains deeply unequal, and that inequality falls hardest on the very people whose communities most need more practitioners.

Upon reflection, I recognise that reducing my fee for Amie had unintended consequences. I may have inadvertently created false expectations, making it more difficult for clients to meet me where I was in terms of professional value, boundaries and sustainability. This tension highlights a broader dilemma, one that cannot be resolved solely at an individual level, particularly given that Black and brown people are disproportionately represented within mental health services and are significantly less likely to receive early, supportive care. Research indicates that Black individuals are overrepresented among in-patients and are more likely to experience compulsory admissions compared to white counterparts. Racialised communities often encounter barriers to accessing timely and culturally appropriate mental health care, leading to disparities in treatment and outcomes (Bhui, Halvorsrud & Nazroo, 2018). There is also significant underrepresentation in psychoanalytic and other mental health professions. Therapy can help explore trauma, yet historically, people of African descent have had limited opportunities to mourn, reflect and heal from the generational impact of slavery, colonialism and other mass atrocities. Focused on day-to-day survival within systems not built for their advancement, Black people are often denied a voice or even a space to think and talk.

Therapy can provide a creative environment where they can be heard and supported. Black people often survive in environments that don't reflect their differences, requiring greater self-sufficiency. Our greatest strength is one another; we need community to help bring the best out of each other. Therapy, including therapy between two Black people, can be a perfect forum for this.

However, there are risks. Both therapist and client can become caught in a shared experience of feeling 'done to', becoming paralysed by a sense of injustice. In these moments, the therapist may absorb some of the client's feelings of not being good enough, creating a complex dynamic where both struggle under the weight of internalised pain.

What started as weekly sessions with Amie would span approximately 18 months, though the frequency would later become a point of contention between us. While our process was slow to get started, this was understandable given the deep-rooted trust issues Amie carried. It wasn't until a few months in that she started to open up about her father who was the source of much of her pain and hesitation.

"He was Muslim," Amie said. This was followed by silence. "He was very religious." Her silence spoke volumes–an emotional breath, a moment to hold the complexity of her father's faith and its impact on her life.

"In what way?" I asked.

"He didn't interact much with us and was always seemed preoccupied with rituals. He also had a recruitment business, all in the outer regions so he was only really around on holidays. He was always going places, or at least, that's how it felt."

Amie and her two younger siblings were born in England; their mother was also English. Her family had lived in Saudi Arabia for a period when she was very young. Her mother eventually returned to England with all three siblings. Her early memories were shaped more by her mother's presence than her father's.

"My mum was always present," Amie said. "We are remarkably close. My dad was in and out of our lives. But he still managed to control my mother in a way I didn't like. One day, he just didn't come back from one of his trips. When the fridge was no longer stacked with food, it turned out he had taken all our money. My mother had three children to look after and no money in the bank!"

"That clearly must have been a difficult time for all of you," I commented.

"After years in a marriage, my mum suddenly had to fend for herself and three children. She already had a job but was forced to take another. She didn't even think twice about it.

Maybe behind the scenes, she remortgaged the house to release some funds."

"You remember this? How old were you?"

"About eight or nine."

"That's quite young. I'm wondering whether that was a scary time for you."

"I wouldn't say scared, exactly, but I was really anxious. I remember Mother was anxious too... she didn't sleep much. She would worry about all sorts of things all the time. If I'm honest, I was more concerned for her than she was of herself."

Amie went on to describe watching her mother struggle to make ends meet. Money was always tight; they couldn't go on school excursions or take holidays. Day-to-day living was strenuous. They survived on essentials, making do with the bare minimum.

"I never want my life to be like that. I can't tell you what that fear is like. I never want to worry about money."

In those early years, her mother's health deteriorated. The doctors could not find the actual cause but asserted that she suffered mainly from malnutrition. Poor living conditions and excessive work made her more susceptible to mental and physical health issues. She was hospitalised numerous times for different heart conditions but managed to pull through all these medical crises. However, she became severely underweight and weak. This experience led Amie to become extremely protective of her.

Amie blamed all these problems on her father. Growing up, he was more of a shadow than a presence, hardly calling or remembering birthdays. As far as she was concerned, he had no regard for their wellbeing. The rare times he did show up, he came bearing gifts that felt more like guilt offerings rather than symbols of genuine affection. Later in her teens, Amie often joked that he had another family back in Saudi Arabia, where he worked for most of his life. Lo and behold, this turned out to be the case.

Then he died.

It wasn't sudden, but it wasn't expected either; he'd had a quiet heart attack overseas. The funeral was small and strange, and afterward came the slow unravelling of everything they thought they knew. In the weeks that followed, while sorting through his documents, bank statements and old correspondence, the truth emerged: he did have another family. A wife. Children. A whole life carefully compartmentalised and kept from them. The joke had become a revelation, and the punchline cut far deeper than anyone had imagined.

"Did his death bring up any unexpected emotions for you?"

Amie blinked at this. "I didn't feel much at all. I didn't like him. What he did was deplorable and irredeemable. I wish he had never been in our lives in the first place. I don't feel guilty saying it."

" He was always mean," Amie continued. "And he was a religious hypocrite. We had to go along with rules, which he flagrantly broke repeatedly. The pressure still follows me around. I did not want to disappoint him, yet he regularly disappointed us. I know that he wanted me to be a high-flyer, like my younger siblings, something like an accountant, lawyer or doctor. He would have been disappointed to know that I'm a dietician!"

For Amie, being the eldest carried its own weight. As the firstborn, she had absorbed the full force of her father's expectations before her siblings were old enough to share them, becoming in effect the test case for everything he hoped his children could achieve. She felt different from her siblings, yet was responsible for them in ways they could never fully understand. In her mind, she was less successful than the others and on top of being the odd one out, she never quite measured up to the standard her father had set. At a deeper level, she buried her worries about her career and instead focused on other ways of gaining praise.

"I figured if I couldn't impress anyone with success, I could at least be useful. So, I made myself available. I remembered every birthday, returned every call and handled every crisis. I became the helper. The one who showed up. I thought maybe that's how love works. You become what people need, and eventually, they'll notice you. They'll love you back, right?"

"Sometimes we learn early on that love is something we have to earn, often by sacrificing parts of ourselves. But real connection doesn't come from being useful. It comes from being known. I wonder what it would feel like to be loved not for what you do, but for who you are."

Amie's need for therapy had been preceded by a mental crisis of sorts. She wasn't sure what had happened. All she knew was that she wanted therapy to help her take more time for herself without always playing the role of the sister and daughter who was responsible for others. Amie hoped our sessions would help her in a quest for change. By improving her mindset, she believed she would improve her financial standing to eventually buy herself and her partner a new car.

I was somewhat sceptical about this. Therapy is rarely about goals or mindset alone; more often, it is about uncovering the internal forces that keep a person locked into self-defeating patterns of behaviour. It is less concerned with what a client wants to achieve and more with what is getting in the way of change.

Amie did not want just any car; she wanted the top-of-the-range Range Rover: sleek, expensive and entirely symbolic. As I came to understand Amie better, I wondered whether her request to pay less was not about affordability. It seemed connected to how she prioritised different aspects of her life, perhaps reflecting deeper conflicts about what she felt she deserved. What she needed was help in learning how to prioritise herself and her intrinsic needs, rather than the relentless responsibility she had carried since childhood, a weight that ambition and constant striving had not lightened but compounded. This ambition was closely linked to Amie's fear of becoming financially destitute like her mother, reckless like her father, and her desire to achieve the kind of stability her siblings appeared to have created in their own lives. At the heart of her trauma was a quest for survival. The disturbance began early, when her sense of security was profoundly shaken, not only by a father who was an inconsistent presence but by a mother who was physically fragile and struggling to make ends meet.

Amie grew up with pervasive anxiety that her security was always at risk, and that money was the only reliable means of safety. Yet I noticed that it was never enough. Her relentless pursuit of more left her dissatisfied and increasingly envious of her siblings, whom she perceived as living more comfortably and successfully.

It was difficult for Amie to recognise that many of her needs were shaped by the expectations of others, especially that of her father; his influence continued to shape how she lived. Over time, she internalised the belief that if she could achieve enough, earn enough, or impress enough, she might finally become worthy of the love and attention that had been missing. That love and attention should have come first from her mother, but she was preoccupied with survival, and from her father, who was similarly preoccupied.

The pursuit of success is not a harmful motivator. But it must come from a place that can be clearly identified as rooted in one's own wants, rather than as an attempt to prove something to others. Beyond that, external markers of success, particularly material things, offer limited and temporary solace. Financial security is important; it allows us to feel safe and stable. But Amie had already achieved this to a reasonable extent. She had a steady job, a regular income and a home she shared with her partner. Her bills were paid, and she could afford frequent holidays. On the surface, there was no immediate threat to her financial wellbeing.

I did not think that buying a new car would suddenly resolve the challenges in her life. Rather, I suspected that the need for more – more wealth, more status and more validation – would simply be transferred onto something else. Therefore, I was not entirely surprised to hear that six months into our work, after she'd secured the car, she needed to save more money for the deposit towards a holiday let. It was at this stage that Amie asked if she could reduce the frequency of our sessions from every week to every fortnight. I could have worked with this if we had been making progress. What dominated our sessions, however, was not self-reflection or emotional insight, it was a striving for ambition and envy. Amie was consumed with the need to be the ideal child and sibling, measuring her worth against those around her.

I countered the request to reduce her sessions by highlighting that we hadn't really started to tackle the issues that resulted in her breakdown. This was what had brought her into therapy in the first place. Although Amie acknowledged that she needed the space to talk about her problems, she admitted that she was struggling to justify the money being spent.

Her relationship with money had become the central theme of our work. She gave a picture of not having enough for therapy but still wanting to continue. It wasn't just about affordability; it was also about value, and where she felt emotionally permitted to invest. I suspected that Amie might stop therapy abruptly because the only way it could work was if I went along with her pretending ours was simply a relationship to help her quest. It had become increasingly clear that, for her, therapy only worked if I aligned myself with her ongoing quest–for status, achievement and external success. Trying to engage her in this bind seemed futile.

Her salary was good and she was on top of her accounts. I could see what money meant to Amie: security, prestige and the means to get what she wanted. Therapy, on the other hand, occupied a more debatable place in her internal value system–justifiable only if it could somehow be linked to earning or achieving more. This made sense if the value was placed on external achievement as opposed to internal security. It struck me that the value of therapy had become the obstacle to getting the life she wanted. It became a bit of a vicious circle.

As our work progressed, Amie became increasingly caught in a familiar pattern–one that mirrored the dynamics that had led to earlier breakdowns. Whenever uncomfortable emotions surfaced, she responded by filling every available space in her life. She took on more work, extended her responsibilities and kept herself constantly occupied, leaving little room for reflection or emotional contact. In addition, her focus shifted towards external markers of success. What began with the desire for a new car evolved into ambitions for larger symbols of achievement, cue the holiday home. These aspirations were not random; they functioned as tangible proof of worth, safety and arrival. Each new goal promised relief, yet the satisfaction it offered was short-lived, quickly giving way to the next objective.

This pattern revealed how success had come to stand in for security and productivity for emotional regulation. By staying busy and striving for more, Amie avoided the vulnerability of acknowledging unmet needs and unresolved loss.

She was disappointed when I declined her request for fortnightly therapy sessions. From her perspective, this support was both necessary and deserved, and if I truly were the loving, caring parent she needed, I would have agreed regardless. Her reaction revealed a part of her that still carried the pain of past deprivation. In her eyes, my refusal to accommodate her was another instance of being denied what she needed, opening old wounds.

I tried to raise this with Amie to explore the earlier losses that had shaped her belief that she needed to remain diligent, reliable and useful. During these discussions, however, she repeatedly returned to the issue of the schedule of her sessions, and I sensed a growing anger towards me. I became the unreasonable one–someone who prioritised financial boundaries over her emotional needs and who failed to recognise that what she needed was important.

Given her history of early deprivation in a deeply unfair world, it was understandable that money had come to represent value, care and recognition. I remained consistent and steady in the therapeutic space, recognising that this dynamic was rooted in Amie's childhood, which had been scarred by deprivation; it was a wound that needed to be tended to many times before mourning and repair could begin.

In many ways, Amie had become hard to reach. She was trapped between long-standing habits of striving and externalising value, and the slower, less predictable nature of therapy, where answers are not immediate and progress not always visible. This frustrated her. Meaning and worth had long been measured through tangible results and therapy offered something far less concrete. Asking her to commit to weekly sessions was not about accelerating her growth, but about inviting her to remain with the uncertainty of the work, rather than retreating into familiar ways of managing discomfort.

Seen in this light, the rupture between us was not caused by the practical issue of session frequency alone, but by what that frequency came to represent. It represented the tension between seeking quick reassurance and tolerating a process that demanded patience, emotional presence and trust in something that could not be immediately proven or measured.

Around 14 months into our work, difficulties that Amie had avoided came to the fore. Her son, who was often in childcare five days a week, no longer called her at night. This struck a chord with her. However difficult it was, it allowed her to consider her feelings beyond financial attainment.

"I don't know what I'm doing. I'm never going to get this time back. I miss my son when I'm at work, but when I get home, all I want to do is sleep so I have enough energy to start again the following day. Is that wrong?"

I wondered whether her son had become a mirror she had not expected. Something of his growing self-sufficiency unsettled her profoundly. The possibility that even her child might not need her in the way she had imagined was not a relief but a quiet devastation.

"A part of you may be reluctant to connect with your partner and son because it could bring up something new about yourself. Spending more time with your son might also mean working less, which could feel difficult. At the same time, you've told me you miss him."

"It's possible that I use work as an escapism."

"I wonder what you're trying to escape from."

"A humdrum lifestyle."

"No one wants that. You don't see value in the life you have currently?"

I then listed what she had going for her–her stable job, her home, her partner, her son–but I didn't think she really took it in. On reflection, I realised this struggle pointed to something deeper: at her core, she had difficulty recognising her own worth. Because she could not fully see value in herself, she also had trouble experiencing the relationships around her as fully affirming. Her connection to her partner or her son was not about them lacking value, but about her inability to receive and feel supported by others without the weight of self-doubt. In other words, if she could not acknowledge her own value, the love and stability offered by those around her risked feeling burdensome rather than sustaining.

"But we wouldn't have any money."

"And you feel you need more money?"

"Well, my partner doesn't mind not having money."

Amie's frustration stemmed from taking on full responsibility for her partner and child in the same way she had with her original family. Internally, it came across as rooted in the distrust that if she did not take responsibility, no one would. Perhaps, in a way, Amie was dealing with the past by taking on the role of what her father should have been–present and responsible. Having committed to a man she perceived as rather incapable and fragile, a dynamic that echoed her relationship with her mother, I understood this fear of lack and this drive. However, I needed her to work out the connection between the past and the present. Given that she was fond of her partner and her son, I wondered if success in that domain would spur her to reconsider what was also important to her.

Amie put a lot of weight on her comparative ambitions. "It's hard to be just a homemaker. Look where it got my mother. And anyway, my siblings all have their own homes and are doing well. I just want to have what they have. It's not a lot to ask for, is it? It just doesn't seem fair. I'm the prettiest, the tallest. I always eat healthy and go to the gym five times a week. But they ended up with bigger houses. I guess they're just lucky."

This was an exposing confession; the quest to have what her siblings had was stopping her from living a life for herself. Amie hated not having been equally successful. When she talked about this, she often looked at me imploringly.

"You're really weighed down by all of that. I understand that it doesn't seem fair. But I'm not sure that acquiring a holiday home is going to give you what you want."

"I'm just trying to do what's needed. I don't feel like I have a choice. I've got to do this."

Soon after, Amie made an offer on the holiday home. Her credit, however, was not good enough to obtain the loan, and she was deeply upset. I empathised with her disappointment. She had worked hard to achieve something she felt would make a change in her life.

Amie perceived the random nature of the home falling through as a personal failing. It led to a dark time; I sensed a shift in her. She became a more distant presence in my consulting room. Her tone turned quite angry. Her failure to get the loan became a failure of the therapy. Still, it gave us an opportunity to slow down even though it meant that we stayed in the depressive state.

Despite all this, Amie continued with her sessions. I wondered why she chose to stay with me, rather than seek someone that might have aligned more easily with her immediate wants–a therapist who offered bi-weekly sessions, or one without the financial constraints our work together carried. My sense was that, on some level, she didn't just want comfort; she also wanted to be challenged, to have someone witness her contradictions without turning away. Amie always described her partner as supportive and the love of her life, but he hardly challenged her. We needed to unpack the idealisation and the defence mechanisms around her relationship narrative.

"You describe your partner as supportive. But does he take on enough responsibility?"

The floodgates opened and everything tumbled out.

"We need to be saving every month," Amie spat out. "But he just doesn't care! I get really stressed out because I'm always the one who sorts everything out while he takes a back seat. Sometimes, I resent him for it. Yes, I carry the burden money-wise between us two."

"Your partner doesn't carry the same desire for wealth. Maybe a part of you envies that."

"I'm resentful because if he stepped up, then I could take a back seat. He doesn't seem to care. And if he did, it would give me a break."

There didn't seem anywhere else to go following that outburst. Her partner was holding her back, apparently, a bit like I was in her eyes. I had the sense that Amie was missing something crucial. Her focus on financial gain and external progress appeared to drown out other needs such as connection, rest, intimacy, play and self-compassion.

Nevertheless, I empathised with Amie's frustration. I could see that she was ambitious, which was part of who she had always been. But I was also curious to know more about what she wanted from her romantic relationship.

"Have you ever shared what you want with him?"

"No. I know what the compromise would be. A small car and definitely not a holiday home. I don't want that."

Bringing up her wants and making an issue of them could potentially threaten the relationship, or worse, destabilise the sense of security within it if she could not compromise. It seemed to me that much remained unspoken in Amie's relationship with her partner. My impression was that he often went along with what she wanted, even though his own desires were simpler, spending time with his family, being present and enjoying ordinary moments. The holiday home became a point of tension: something Amie wanted yet also struggled to actually get.

However, over the coming weeks, Amie was able to recognise that her behaviour, i.e., her obsession with work and money was driving a wedge between her and her partner.

"We used to have a really close bond but now it's slowly coming apart. Probably it's me being relentless," she chuckled, shaking her head slightly.

I smiled in response, letting the comment hang in the space between us.

"I don't know. I mean, I pay for most things. Holidays, bills, rent," she added, her voice tinged with a mixture of pride and frustration.

"Is that something you want to do?" I asked, leaning forwards slightly.

"It made sense at first because our place was initially mine. He came to live with me and I was already paying the bills. I suppose I just carried on," she shrugged, a faint smile flickering across her face.

"Do you think asking him to contribute more would help?" I prompted gently.

She paused, tapping her fingers on the arm of her chair. "I could maybe ask him to pay for our holiday," she said slowly, as if testing the idea out loud.

"I think he will agree, but he won't be entirely happy about it. He'll probably complain about how much it all costs." Amie laughed, a short, bright chuckle that seemed to ease some of the tension in the room.

Soon after this session, she went for a holiday with her family and they reconnected in ways that did her good. She returned less stressed, having stepped back from financial responsibility and from the pressures she carried at home.

Therapy requires commitment and continuity. Clients book the therapist's time and expertise, and the work is sustained both in sessions and in the therapist's ongoing care in between those sessions. The financial contract reinforces the value of this work and it is part of the framework alongside time, space and the therapeutic relationship. Unlike tangible purchases, therapy asks clients to invest in something internal: growth, understanding and emotional repair.

Meaningful change emerges only when there is a genuine willingness to engage with the process. Through sustained participation, clients come to realise that the true gains cannot be measured in monetary terms. What they find instead is something far greater: a deeper sense of self, healing and connection. Therapists who have undergone their own work know this first-hand; the value of therapy extends well beyond what can be bought or quantified.

Our work ended after 18 months, not with a planned termination but with Amie's decision that she could no longer afford weekly sessions. Despite our exploration of what this decision meant – another loss, another abandonment, another instance of having to choose between competing needs – she felt the financial burden was too great. I wondered if this ending replicated something familiar: leaving before being left, and choosing deprivation over dependence. We spoke about her returning when circumstances changed, but I haven't heard from her since. The therapy ended as it had begun – with money standing between us, representing everything we'd tried to work through but couldn't quite resolve.

Working with Amie taught me how complicated it can be when issues of money, race and access intersect in the therapy room. My decision to reduce my fee came from a genuine commitment to making therapy more accessible, particularly for Black clients who face structural barriers to mental healthcare. But I learned that good intentions don't always lead to straightforward outcomes.

This case reminded me that individual therapists cannot solve what requires systemic change through sliding scales. We need better funding for mental healthcare, more diversity in the profession and structural support for therapists who want to work accessibly without undermining their own sustainability. Until then, we navigate these tensions as best we can, knowing that every decision about fees and boundaries carries meaning that extends far beyond the practical.

Frank: Masculinity, Vulnerability and Authority

I took an immediate liking to Frank, a fair-skinned, mixed-heritage Black man with a boyish appearance. His hair, worn in brown locks, was often tied back in a topknot. One week he would appear smart in a polo shirt and slacks; the next, he wore colourful, mismatched clothes. His outward presentation, like much about him, seemed changeable, and it was a reflection of the uncertainty he carried inside.

"I don't know my own mind," Frank started. "I can't decide what to do with my career or personal relationships."

I listened, trying to form a picture in my mind of who he was and what was going on for him at that point in his life. As he spoke, I imagined the weight of his days–how they seemed to blur together, each one indistinct from the last. His voice carried a tired honesty, the kind that comes from sitting with the same feelings for too long.

"I feel down most of the time," he said. "Sort of… unsettled. Lacking direction."

There was a pause after his words, as if even he wasn't sure how to fill the space they left behind.

From the outset, I noticed that the clothes he wore were almost a caricature, like exaggerations rather than expressions of who he was. As time went on, it felt as though he was trying out different versions of Frank, experimenting with how he might be seen. At times his appearance leaned towards the humorous or theatrical, giving the impression of someone light-hearted and fun.

Yet this outward playfulness sat uneasily beside the internal emotional tone he had initially described. There was a quiet dissonance between what he showed and what he felt. His visual cues suggested an ease and whimsy, while his words pointed to something heavier and more unsettled. The two didn't quite align.

I was struck by Frank's youthfulness. He had what we might call 'a baby face.' From our early interactions, his overall presence seemed younger than his 36 years; he was full of impulsive energy and emotionally unformed. He still had that lost, carefree sensibility of a student, or somebody in their late teens. There was something vulnerable and disoriented about him that evoked in me a powerful maternal response.

We started working together in the spring of 2018. What started as weekly sessions would continue for nearly four years.

"It's so great to find a Black therapist." This was nice to hear from a client. I felt the compliment was genuine. "I've been looking for one, a Black female therapist, for a long time."

"What are you hoping to get from this space?" I asked with genuine curiosity as to what my racial and gender identity might mean to him.

"If I had a male therapist, I would feel too restrained, possibly ashamed to say what I really felt. I mean, I'm hardly the masculine epitome. I can't believe I am confessing this, but I'm intimidated around other Black men. I don't fit in the 'strong Black male' stereotype. In fact, I'm not sure where I fit."

Frank spoke about a preference to be taller as he did not seem content with an average build. I wondered instead if he was missing a role model worth emulating. Our session felt very personal–more so than usual. I was struck by how much attention Frank gave to his physical appearance, which I saw as wiry; it was as if his body was carrying meaning about how he saw himself. A few questions stayed with me afterwards. What was Frank's definition of masculinity? Who represented that definition for him? What or who was shaping that image?

I found myself thinking that his understanding of masculinity may have been influenced by internalised figures and wider cultural expectations, such as the idea of the 'alpha male. Maybe he aspired to an external ideal of masculinity which could lead to dissatisfaction if it felt out of reach or was constantly changing. At the same time, I was aware that masculinity is shaped not only by personal experience but also by social and symbolic pressures. Perhaps Frank's focus on his physicality was a way of trying to ground or define himself within these influences. This left me reflecting on masculinity as something fluid and relational, shaped over time through both inner experience and external expectations.

We talked a lot in those early sessions. Despite this, Frank did not really engage. He spoke in a rambling manner or very quickly when excited, which made him difficult to understand. I struggled to stay fully present and to find the essence of him. Perhaps this performative style came from a deeper belief that he couldn't be met as he truly was, that simply showing up as his unguarded self wouldn't be enough. I found myself wondering whether he might have felt that I wasn't genuinely interested in him, and that this urge to perform was, in some way, an attempt to bridge that imagined distance.

Frank frowned. "I'm not sure what to say. What am I supposed to say? Like… in therapy generally?"

Even though Frank liked coming for his sessions, I sensed that alongside his attempts to entertain or deflect, he also felt that something was expected of him and as such, he wasn't sure how to use the therapy space. I thought this had a wider resonance. It spoke to something around his feelings in new spaces and relating to others generally.

I also empathised with Frank's uncertainty. At the beginning of any therapeutic process, it is not uncommon for clients to feel unsure about how, or even where to begin. Frank seemed to carry a sense that there was something specific expected of him, as though he were meant to arrive with the right words or a clearly defined problem, rather than allowing the work to unfold gradually.

Sensing this, I offered a lifeline. "As with most new relationships, we are trying to find our way. It's a process that unfolds over time. There is no right or wrong way. Maybe there are questions I can ask that might help you get in touch with your feelings and thoughts."

"Okay, like what?"

"Well, how about you start by telling me about yourself–your family or your upbringing." I hoped this would help him find his footing. Talking about family often opened doors to understanding how we relate to others and how we see ourselves.

Frank told the story of his early life in a very meandering way over several sessions. I often found it extremely difficult to follow the thread. He would divert and cut back, rather than keep to the point at hand. I'll provide a summary here, rather than attempt to render this patchwork of anecdotes, into something orderly.

Frank had spent some of his childhood in Italy. There, his mother, who was white British, had met his father who was

Black British. His father worked for the government and was posted to Italy; at least, that is what he had been told.

He shared that for much of his childhood he believed he shared the same father with his older sister. It wasn't until the age of 14 that he was told–somewhat abruptly and in a matter-of-fact way–that he had different fathers. This revelation was shocking and emotionally destabilising, and he found it difficult to fully assimilate the details.

Frank recalled the moment he learned about his father's identity. From the way it was revealed, as an off-hand comment slipped into a casual moment, offered without eye contact, emotional acknowledgement, or any invitation for questions, he immediately sensed there was something shameful about the truth. The detached, almost careless tone suggested that his father's identity, and perhaps even the circumstances of his conception, were not things to be spoken about openly. Although the words themselves were delivered casually, the news landed heavily. What stayed with Frank was not only what he had been told, but how it had been said: as if minimising the moment might contain its discomfort or keep something unspoken safely buried.

As a result of the sense of shame that he had picked up on, he lost trust in his mother and his sister. It upset me to hear Frank refer to himself as a 'bastard', or as someone no one wanted. He resented his mother for having lied to him and for singling him out as different. She worked at a bakery factory and often worked night shifts. And when she wasn't working, she would stay over at her then-boyfriend's place.

Frank's mother had always claimed that his father left when she became pregnant. He couldn't understand why a man would want to leave his unborn child. He oscillated between wanting to find him and not, perhaps afraid of the unknown. Nonetheless, he often wondered what it would be like to know his father. His mother had also explained that his father was not looking for anything serious. However, he couldn't understand how she could fall for someone who did not value her enough to build a relationship with her. To him, she had been negligent. Throughout his childhood, she'd had several partners, but most of them, he felt, were far from suitable father figures. Instead, they were men who came to take but never to stay.

As a result, he was often left to his own devices, and for as far back as he could remember, he largely catered to himself. His sister was around until she became interested in boys, and after that, she was rarely home. Frank spent much of his time watching TV, taking long walks or hanging out with friends. Those early years seemed to shape him in subtle but lasting ways. As a result, he developed a nonchalant, sarcastic exterior which was in fact a protective layer shielding a more fragile inner self. Rather than dwelling on his isolation, he often gravitated towards groups of friends, using their company as both distraction and defence.

From the beginning, it became clear that Frank's relationship with his mother was deeply complex marked by ambivalence, emotional distance and intermittent tender moments that were soon overshadowed by inconsistency. She was not entirely absent nor overtly cruel, but her love seemed unpredictable and at times withdrawn. Frank both loved and resented her, a tension that surfaced frequently in therapy. His attachment to her appeared to be shaped by a persistent hope that she might one day meet him emotionally, while also carrying the pain of repeated disappointment. This emotional push and pull seemed to mirror how Frank navigated other relationships: with caution, craving and confusion.

After high school, Frank got into trouble for minor misdemeanours such as burglaries. His mother kicked him out of the house, leaving him to fend for himself–a rejection that carried echoes of earlier losses and absences, particularly the unresolved questions surrounding his father. During this precarious period, Frank eventually secured an apprenticeship as a locksmith. Over time, he carved out a modicum of comfort and a surface-level stability. There's no doubt this speaks to a quiet resilience: an ability to adapt, survive and keep moving forwards despite inconsistent emotional support.

Yet even as he settled into that role, restlessness lingered beneath the surface. He described everything as feeling temporary, as if he were forever anticipating the next thing; never fully rooted and never quite settled. His early experiences of abandonment, compounded by repeated rejection, left a shadow that resilience alone could not erase.

In his early 20s, he became drawn to the glitzy life of London. The city's energy, its diversity and the constant movement spoke to something in him – a desire to connect, to belong and to be part of something bigger than the small, fractured worlds he had known. Moving to London felt like a chance to start anew. For the first time, he felt a measure of acceptance. There was a freedom in the cultural mix, a sense of difference that was celebrated rather than judged, and for a while, he could inhabit that space without the weight of past rejections pressing in.

In addition to what I had already observed, I became aware that, as the only Black person currently present in Frank's life, I sometimes came to symbolise aspects of the absent Black father. Within him, this figure was idealised as someone who might step forwards, make things right, and redeem the past. At the same time, that same father figure could evoke deep anger: for his abandonment, his silence and the betrayal of having fathered a child out of wedlock before disappearing into the shadows. In this dynamic, I found myself occupying, in part, the position of that idealised father: stable, reliable, nurturing and capable of offering structure and guidance. These were qualities that reflected an unresolved need within him.

Yet as a woman, I also appeared to represent something akin to an idealised and at times denigrated female/mother figure. I praised his efforts, offered affirmation and provided encouragement–things he had so often been denied in childhood. I noticed that he responded with visible relief, as though something long starved in him was finally being fed. My presence seemed to activate both longing and defensiveness, the simultaneous pull of comfort and unresolved tension, highlighting the complex ways he related to figures of care and authority. At times, he responded with warmth and openness, but at others, he subtly dismissed or undermined my interventions, as though minimising my support or testing whether it was genuine. These patterns of idealisation and devaluation reflected his early relational experiences and a wariness of closeness that carried the risk of disappointment or hurt.

Over time, Frank and I were able to create a consistent and reliable space. It was a place where he could begin to explore, at his own pace, not only his feelings and relationships but also who he was and who he wanted to become.

The psychoanalyst Donald Winnicott wrote about the importance of what he called a 'holding environment', or a safe space where someone can explore who they are without fear of rejection or abandonment (1971). Our therapy room needed to become that for Frank. Within this space, he could experiment with aspects of himself that had long been constrained by past rejection or the need to perform. He began to try out being more open and vulnerable, testing trust in ways he had rarely allowed himself. Then he explored ambition and responsibility without the fear of judgment; practised self-compassion rather than self-criticism; and even allowed himself moments of joy without immediately downplaying them.

About 18 months into our work, Frank shared that he had recently met someone at a coffee shop. His eyes lit up slightly as he recounted the encounter, a rare spark of animation breaking through his usual guarded demeanour.

"I was flattered by her," he said, a small smile tugging at the corners of his mouth. "She came on to me and seemed to like my humour. So, we started talking and shortly afterwards dating."

There was a hint of excitement in his voice, mixed with an undercurrent of disbelief, as if he could hardly believe things were going well.

"After that, everything moved fast. She asked me to move in with her." He shrugged, half amused, half anxious, as though trying to gauge how he was meant to feel about this sudden shift in his life.

The rapid pace of the relationship also surprised me. It seemed to echo earlier themes of a longing to be seen, valued and wanted, alongside the vulnerability that comes with such intensity. I found myself wondering how Frank navigated closeness and trust, particularly in the context of a self that was still emerging and finding shape.

"Did you like her?"

He paused, thoughtful, his gaze dropping briefly before meeting mine again.

"You know… I'm not sure, to be honest. She wanted to look after me and offer a place to stay and just… be nice. That was kind of attractive."

"And now?" I asked gently, picking up on the same hesitancy, wanting to give him space to reflect.

"Well… it worked for a while. But she didn't want to tell her parents about being in an interracial relationship. I felt like a dirty little secret."

He gave a half-smile, almost apologetic, as if acknowledging both the reality and the awkwardness of his feelings. There was a flicker of hurt in his eyes, tempered by a touch of self-conscious humour, revealing the complex mix of longing for connection and the sting of exclusion.

"To be honest, at first, I didn't mind the 'parents thing.' It wasn't really a big deal. But then I began to feel restless. I got tired of it. There was just something repetitive and mundane about our day-to-day living."

"What was it you hoped for?"

There was something familiar in the way he described being hidden that resonated with the shame he carried about not being fully wanted by his father, and perhaps even by his mother. Being the 'secret' in the relationship seemed to reactivate that early wound. He looked down at his hands.

"I really don't know. I guess I hoped for more, though I can't say exactly what. Maybe I imagined it differently, more fun. I also admit I just get restless, and then I find myself thinking about going back to Italy, back to what feels familiar and safe, even if it's not exactly what I want."

"Italy being a return to something you know?"

"I guess...," Frank looked up at the ceiling. A few emotions played across his face. These emotions were difficult to read. Wistfulness, perhaps? Sadness mixed with hope?

On the surface, he had managed to build a functional life, but beneath that lay a persistent invisibility. He struggled with rootlessness, uncertainty about what he truly wanted and a longing for belonging that he couldn't quite name.

"I guess for me, home is more like an idea than an actual place. It's somewhere you belong. Somewhere you're accepted."

"And do you feel like you have ever lived out this idea?"

"I've never had anything like that. But I guess you could say that's what I want. Back in Italy, I would say that at least I knew what to expect. This may sound bleak but at the same time, I didn't have high expectations. It was familiar. And yeah, it was a bit shit at times."

"It's often better in fantasy."

"That's right. I sometimes think I want something different from my mother. I both love and resent her. But, as you said, reality is often different from what we imagine. When I'm back there, I'm reminded of what life used to be like. Still, I have my cat."

He went on to tell me about Tabby, his cat, who was then 13 years old. He got her when he was a teenager; in fact, around the same time he found out about his father. Tabby arrived at a moment when his world felt destabilised, offering a small, steady presence amid the upheaval.

"Cats offer comfort," Frank had said.

Tabby's presence seemed to have taken on a deeper, more symbolic role. She offered Frank the constancy, warmth and emotional safety he couldn't receive from the adults in his life.

"Yes, they do. I like my cat; she is very consistent," I affirmed Frank's observation.

He paused, his gaze drifting for a moment as if weighing memories against the present. The corners of his mouth softened into a faint, almost imperceptible smile.

"It wasn't all bad. My mother always said that I could do anything if I put my mind to it. To be honest, I've always believed that too. If given a shot, I could achieve anything – even when the odds seemed stacked against me."

"She saw something in you."

"Yes, that's right. And she made me see it, too."

I sat back in the chair, quietly pleased. I was seeing Frank liven up; there was an energy in him, as though the memory of being seen, truly seen, had momentarily lifted something heavy from his shoulders. There was a glimpse of vitality, of self-belief trying to take root.

"You then made it in the kitchen," I said.

"I've always been interested in food, maybe because my mother didn't cook. I learnt by watching cookery programmes on TV. It was something I did for her, so she'd have something to eat before and after work. It was inevitable, I guess, that I ended up in the kitchens. When I arrived in London, I managed to get a job at Carlo's, a little Italian restaurant. I couldn't cook much at first – I winged it in the beginning – but I've always been willing to learn. I remember my mother's voice saying, 'You can do anything you put your mind to.' So, I put my mind to it. And now… I'm pretty good."

In previous sessions, Frank had explained how, in this first job, working for a small family business, he felt as though he was part of the team. It had been difficult to leave, as he had finally found that essential thing he was driven towards – belonging. But he wanted more; he wanted to explore what England could provide. Frank moved on from this first job after serving an apprenticeship.

Over the next two years, with qualifications and demonstrable cookery skills, he worked his way up through the restaurant industry in London. Hardworking and methodical, he grew into a technically expert chef. And by the time we reached the middle years of our work together, as the head chef of a small group, he was lauded and praised. Highly commended for his creativity and ability, he'd risen to a managerial role, with responsibilities for two restaurants in that group.

Frank had invited me to his restaurant, and I was genuinely pleased, though of course I couldn't accept; he was my client. Nevertheless, it was a lovely offer. I told him that under different circumstances, I would have been glad to go. I could sense how proud he was, and I felt pleased to know that he wanted to share something of his life with me.

Each promotion made him hungry for more. He worked hard and progressed quickly, driven not just by ambition but by a need to be taken seriously. At work, he achieved that recognition. Yet the qualities he displayed professionally of self-discipline, focus, determination were often absent in his personal life.

The purpose of our work was to help Frank recognise and reflect on this divide between how he functioned in different areas of his life. It wasn't just a matter of behaviour; it was about identity. Understanding the person he presented to the world versus the person he experienced in private. Humour was one of Frank's most obvious skills, and not just for laughs. He used it to connect with others, to lighten the mood and to make himself approachable; but it was also a shield. When conversations brushed too close to his vulnerabilities, humour allowed him to deflect and to control the interaction without exposing too much of himself.

In many ways, it was a habit he'd learned early as a way to manage the tension between what he wanted and what he felt safe revealing. Jokes allowed him to engage socially while keeping people at a comfortable distance. They also signalled that his words shouldn't be taken too seriously, a subtle way of protecting himself from judgment or rejection. The tricky part was that, while humour made Frank likeable and adaptable, it also left gaps. People laughed with him but rarely saw the parts of him that were uncertain, restless or deeply reflective. Behind the quick wit and self-deprecating jokes, much remained unspoken. In essence, humour gave him a way to navigate the world, but at the cost of being truly known, both by others and, at times, even by himself.

Frank had never let anyone get close to him. He had close friends in Italy, but none in the UK. Neither had he ever depended on anyone. Another use of humour was to get the many benefits of friendship, but without the potential risks. If you don't make yourself vulnerable, if you don't take the risk of letting people into your life, you pre-emptively avoid the disappointment of their departure or absence. So, sensing the conflict between his wish to be close coupled with his fear of what closeness might mean, I thought it would be helpful to state my position.

"Part of you seems curious about getting closer to this work, and another part seems unsure about what that might lead to. I want you to know that I'm committed to working through that with you."

Frank chuckled. "I agree with you. I don't feel I'm ready to stop now either."

Around the two-and-a-half-year mark, Frank shared with me that he identified as polysexual. This disclosure seemed to mark a turning point, not only in our work but in his relationship with himself. He used the terms polysexual and queer intermittently, which to me felt like part of a broader process of self-discovery and exploration of belonging. It seemed that his chosen sexual objects are linked to identification with who he feels drawn to, reflected in or connected with rather than fitting neatly into societal categories. This stood in contrast to conventional ways of thinking about sexuality, which often feel rigid or homophobic, prescribing desire based on gender rather than experience.

But alongside this new clarity came a familiar discomfort. Shame lingered just beneath the surface, shame about how he might be perceived and about not fitting into dominant expectations of masculinity or sexuality. His journey of naming his desires and identity reflects both a movement towards authenticity and the ongoing tension of negotiating societal pressures versus personal truth.

Around the same time, he brought up his father again; he had spoken intermittently about him. He thought about finding him and if he did, whether it was worth trying to get to know him. When the subject arose, he expressed ambivalence–curiosity mixed with doubt and uncertainty. In those moments, I acknowledged that we could not know in advance how such an encounter might unfold. It might offer clarity or a sense of connection, but it could also reopen old wounds or introduce new complexities.

It seemed to me that Frank's wish to reach out was less about reconciliation in a conventional sense and more about a desire for recognition and acceptance; a hope that his father might see him, validate his experiences or bear witness to who he has become. I also needed him to know, as his therapist, my belief that gender and sexuality are not always aligned, and that identity–like race–is shaped by many factors, including personal experience, reflection, and what one makes of it. Whatever choice he made, my role was to hold space and to remain alongside him as he considered the possibilities. I was reminded that identity is fluid and complex, and that our sense of self is shaped through ongoing relational experiences.

Over the following year, I noticed positive changes in Frank. He had been naïve in manner, seemingly floating through life. Gradually, he began to take more personal interest in health and wellbeing. With each passing week, he looked and felt more attractive and self-assured. He was beginning to tolerate uncertainty more fully. Rather than rushing to resolve tension through humour or explanation, he was able to remain with his ambivalence. Silence no longer had to be filled, but something that could be held. This suggested a developing capacity to think rather than perform in the therapeutic space.

In Frank's case, progress was less about direction and more about containment. Having a space where uncertainty could be held without pressure allowed him to think more freely and act more deliberately. Every time a client retells a story from their past, the details are presented somewhat differently, adding something else. It's a process of remembering. This is why we revisit the past many times over.

As Frank retold the story of his early life, new insights began to emerge. Growing up as a mixed-heritage child in a predominantly white environment meant that he encountered both overt and subtle forms of racism. Most of the time, he described this as a persistent feeling of difference. It was one that became, in his words, 'a kind of handicap, something he had learned to function within rather than question. He spoke about the shame of growing up feeling and looking different. This sense of exposure was heightened by the remoteness of the village where they lived, where standing out was unavoidable and anonymity impossible. Frank reflected that instinctively he had believed that if a father had been present–visibly part of the family unit–he might have felt more protected. A father, he imagined, could have served as a buffer against the looks of judgment and the unspoken questions about who he was and where he belonged.

"Did you share this with your mother?" I asked.

"Yes, she was sort of supportive," Frank said. "She would say, 'You're handsome; don't mind them'." He paused, his expression tightening slightly as if he were replaying those moments rather than simply recalling them. "But, you know, I think in a way that side-lined what I was actually feeling and seeing. I couldn't just ignore it."

"You wanted her to engage."

"Yes! She could've started by reading all the books out there about these issues. It's shameful to have a mixed-heritage son and not know anything about Black history."

Frank was angry and frustrated, understandably. He'd given a heartfelt account of his experience. It seemed likely that, at some level, his mother recognised what was going on. Her responses, though perhaps well-meaning, carried a kind of denial, as if naming racism, shame, or difference might somehow make it more real. But of course, the opposite was true. By dismissing his experience, she left him alone with it. This conversation brought up the question of finding his father again. It struck me that it was not so much the father Frank wanted, but what the father represented. It created a space in which we could think together about what that relationship stood for. It became clear that what Frank was yearning for was not the father *per se*, but something more fundamental: the desire to be seen, validated and understood in the full complexity of his identity.

Could his white mother have fulfilled this role? I believe she could have, at least in part. Frank was not seeking acceptance from the racist 'Other,' but rather from her, his primary caregiver and his mother. That kind of recognition would have required her to enter emotional and political territory: to show not only a willingness to understand and empathise, but to actively stand up for him when needed. That, to me, is what true allyship looks like. Her silence or avoidance around race functioned as a kind of erasure.

Frank couldn't reconcile the different aspects of his identities, i.e., being Black and being polysexual. It was as if the two identities clashed inside him, not because they were inherently incompatible, but because of how the world saw them. I found myself desperately wanting Frank to overcome these societal stigmas. A polysexual man, especially a Black man, is so often misunderstood, sexualised, or dismissed. Society doesn't quite know what to do with someone like Frank. To some, he's threatening; to others, a curiosity. Rarely is he simply allowed to be

Towards the end of our work, Frank gradually began to seek out and form friendships with other Black gay men. This emerged not as a sudden change, but as a tentative and increasingly confident movement towards relationships in which aspects of his identity no longer needed to be explained or defended. These friendships offered a form of recognition and mirroring that had been largely absent in his early family relationships, allowing him to feel seen and validated in ways that previously felt unreachable. In these spaces, he told me he felt more at home.

Frank experienced an authentic feeling not felt before–an ease in being seen, recognised and understood without the need for explanation or performance. There was a shared language, both spoken and unspoken, that made these relationships feel grounding. He was no longer trying to reconcile parts of himself in isolation but instead finding mirrors in others who held similar complexities. His experience existed at a series of intersections that offered few role models and even fewer spaces of full belonging. Black men like Frank are in the process of redefining masculinity and sexuality–doing the hard work of rebuilding these identities on their own terms, without a script and with little precedent. At times, this process looked like uncertainty, like not knowing.

It is understandable, then, that when identity is not clear-cut, individuals may seek external validation and belonging through collective identities. For some young Black men, gangs can appear to offer a sense of belonging and a framework for identity formation. However, without guidance or space to embrace the full humanity of their emotions and vulnerabilities, this search for belonging can lead to the re-enactment of the very oppression they have experienced. As a result, some young Black men can become entangled in criminal activity and, subsequently, end up in the criminal justice system.

Still, despite the stereotype, there is an incredible vulnerability among Black men, which often goes unrecognised, both by themselves and by others. This vulnerability can be external, as in encounters with policing, or internal, as in Frank's struggle to lower his guard. When one is caught in a system that demonises them, maintaining dignity becomes profoundly difficult. Ziauddin Sardar, in his foreword to *Black Skin, White Masks*, characterises Fanon's project as a quest for Black men to be themselves in all their multiplicities (Sardar, 2008). By this, Fanon pointed to the radical idea that Black men should be free to exist as complex, layered and full human beings, and not as flattened, controlled, or narrowly defined versions of themselves imposed by societal expectations. Frank's journey reflected this struggle: to exist fully, in all his complexity, despite the expectations and stereotypes of society.

There was no 'aha!' moment for Frank. He didn't arrive at a neat and satisfactory conclusion. His was not an overnight success. He didn't wake up one day with all the answers. He also didn't change dramatically, nor did he miraculously get a pre-packaged answer to the question of who he wanted to be. Rather, he changed in small ways over the years with me, surprising himself as we went along. More importantly, he became more accepting of his identity.

In my view, Frank managed to, as they say, 'do the work.' Though he was still searching for something, most of us are – he wasn't pinning all his hopes on a reconciliation with his father. Instead, he remained open to the opportunities that life could offer for a better future. Frank actively worked towards that idea of home. Indeed, he set about creating this home for himself, starting from where he was, rather than hoping to stumble across it elsewhere by constantly moving on.

As time went by, Frank reported feeling more content. He also developed interests beyond his job, stepping out of his comfort zone by trying gigs as a stand-up comic, specialising in imitations. In his quest for stability, he allowed himself the right to stay in one place, saving enough money to buy a house, an incredible life achievement and a traditional marker of adulthood. He was no longer searching for a home; he had created one for himself. He was no longer directionless or aimless. He had become the sharp-suited, respected, trusted, yet still caring and hilarious man he had always wanted to be.

Nearly four years after we'd met, Frank and I initiated discussions on winding things down. Towards the end of our time together, I looked up at Frank one day and remarked on how different he seemed. He radiated a wonderful sense of solidity and stability – a vision of a different kind of masculinity, one that suited him perfectly. Even his outfit reflected this shift. Gone were the overly playful, performative styles he had once worn, the outfits that sometimes felt like caricatures, as though he was still trying on different versions of himself. Now, he dressed in a way that aligned with who he was becoming – understated but intentional, comfortable yet confident. There was a coherence between his inner and outer self that had not always been present.

Whatever happened with his father at this stage, I knew he would be fine. I felt incredibly proud of Frank. He had overcome so much, travelled so far and become so very impressive.

In the end, he found the right point for us to leave things.

"Abi, whenever I don't know what to do, I just think to myself, 'What would Abi say about this?' And that helps."

I was deeply touched; it was heart-warming to hear such a compliment. He had internalised something stabilising through the work we had done together. Frank taught me that identity isn't something you discover all at once. It's something you build, gradually, through relationships where you feel safe enough to try being yourself. He'd arrived in my therapy room without a clear sense of who he was or where he belonged. This wasn't because he lacked ability or insight, but because the foundational relationships that typically help us develop a coherent sense of self had been unstable or absent. His father had disappeared before he was born, his mother's care was inconsistent, and the revelation about his paternity as a teen shattered what little certainty he had. What struck me most was how Frank had learned to survive by performing rather than being. His humour, his charm, even his wardrobe – these were all ways of staying visible while remaining hidden. He could engage with the world without risking genuine connection, protecting himself from the rejection he'd come to expect.

As a Black female therapist, I was aware that I represented something significant for Frank. I embodied aspects of both the absent Black father he idealised and longed for, and the consistent mother figure he'd never quite had. This dual identification – being both the father who might finally see him and the mother who might finally stay – meant our relationship carried weight. I had to be mindful not to overidentify with his experiences while still offering the recognition he needed.

Conclusion

I wrote this book for several reasons. The first was to give a voice and witness to my brother, Adebayo. From his teens to the time of his death at 41, he was consistently failed by a mental health system that could not see him, hear him, or value him.

The second was that I believe that there are aspects of psychotherapy that can transform lives and mental health, but only if the field itself transforms. The field needs individuals from diverse backgrounds who can each bring their unique perspectives to the work. Psychotherapy cannot remain the domain of a privileged few if it is to truly serve the many.

The third was to speak to Black women because, as one myself, I experience the struggle. I am acutely aware of the intersectionality that shapes our lives – the compounded weight of racism and sexism, the burden of misogynoir that renders us simultaneously hypervisible and invisible, and the dissonance that comes with being valued for our labour yet devalued in our personhood. Misogynoir shapes not only how we are seen by the world but how we are permitted to see ourselves. The stereotypes of the angry Black woman, the strong Black woman who needs no support and the mammy who exists to nurture others become psychological constraints that dictate what feelings are allowed, needs can be expressed and versions of self are deemed acceptable. In contrast, I believe that Black women are powerful beyond measure. We carry histories of resistance, creativity and survival. We hold knowledge that has been systematically excluded from therapeutic discourse, yet it is precisely this knowledge that could reshape the field entirely.

Next, I wrote this book for my Black clients and Black trainee therapists who started their programs eager to learn, only to find themselves just as eager to finish. Why? Because the psychotherapy they encounter has not considered their difference, offers no space for them to bring their whole selves into the room, treats their cultural knowledge as a deficit rather than a resource, and makes them translate themselves into frameworks built without them in mind.

I also wrote this book to interrogate whiteness to show how it operates not just in overt discrimination but in the subtle architecture of therapeutic theory itself. It means that good intentions are not enough without structural critique, and that they must reckon with their own implication in systems they seek to dismantle.

Finally, I wrote this book to give countless others a voice and an understanding that the forces at play are many and complex and that trauma does not need to define them. It is my firm belief that difference doesn't need to divide us. With enough curiosity, difference attracts. There is so much to be learned from one another.

These convictions did not arrive fully formed. They emerged through years of practice, loss and reckoning with what psychotherapy claims to offer and what it delivers. Early in my career, I sought training hoping for a roadmap to understanding others. What I discovered was that no such schematic exists. Psychotherapy, like life, is not a step-by-step process but an experience to be lived, something that changes us as we move through it.

Each journey is unique, shaped by history, identity and perspective. What I brought to training was my own history, my own identity, my own perspective; and what I took away was shaped by that. My training was by default different to everyone else's because *I* am different. No universal formula exists, only curiosity, presence and a willingness to engage fully with the person before you.

Training gave me skills–emotional insight, relational sensitivity and the capacity to sit with discomfort, both my own and that of my clients. Yet the deeper lesson was that therapy is always a dialogue between two individuals, each carrying their own histories, assumptions and blind spots. This work exposes our limitations and biases, yet it remains profoundly rewarding. The act of bearing witness, listening without judgment, naming injustice, recognising achievement, and holding vulnerability, allows both client and therapist to see themselves differently, more fully, and with greater compassion.

I believe that doing this work would benefit those trying to gain an understanding of their lives. Training to become a psychotherapist forces us to reflect on our make-up, our assumptions and blind spots. In doing so, we gain greater insight into the positions of others; by challenging the things we hold as self-evident, we improve our capacity to empathise. This, then, is the contradiction at the heart of psychotherapy, and at the heart of being human: we cannot understand, let alone help others, when we haven't started the process of understanding ourselves.

At its core, psychotherapy is about making the unconscious conscious. We uncover the patterns that shape our lives–the fears, beliefs and habits often invisible even to ourselves. These patterns are deeply entwined with history, culture, race and social structures. A person's suffering cannot be separated from the world they inhabit, and the therapist's role is to meet them there–with openness, curiosity and humility. When we create space to speak openly, without judgment, these patterns begin to emerge, creating pathways towards insight and transformation.

Psychoanalysis offers valuable tools for this work. The work is understanding that we all have thoughts and feelings we're not fully aware of; that early relationships shape who we become; that we repeat patterns without realising it; and that talking openly can help bring those patterns to light. These principles can be applied to anyone because they address universal aspects of human experience–emotion, relationships and the search for meaning.

The therapist must be available to hear, to make something of what is being told, to help process it with the client, and to support them through to recovery. This requires deep listening, empathy, reflective questioning, and creating a safe, non-judgmental space. Most crucially, it requires an understanding of the client's struggles as fundamentally human problems, not just symptoms to be diagnosed, and approaching them with genuine curiosity rather than pathologising.

Therapy alone is never enough. Or, more precisely, it opens doors rather than providing destinations. True wellbeing demands attention to the body, to the rhythms of daily life and to the social and political contexts that shape our existence. Some arrive at therapy with the hope that being 'therapeutised' will itself constitute cure. But therapy, at its best, cultivates awareness–awareness of the broader terrain of one's life and the multiple pathways towards change that exist beyond the consulting room.

Over 16 years of practice, I have learned that healing, when it comes, is holistic. My work has been shaped not only by psychoanalysis but by Black feminist thought, by music and art, by somatic practices including mindfulness, meditation, yoga, acupuncture and breathwork.

Psychoanalysis is not the whole story, nor should it be treated as such. The call to decolonise the curriculum remains vital, and while institutional change may or may not come, we cannot afford to wait. We must take what serves us and challenge what does not, claiming the authority to practise in ways that honour the fullness of human experience.

The persistent impact of racism runs through all of this. But so too does homophobia, Islamophobia and all the other systems of oppression that people struggle against daily. Constant exposure to stereotyping, discrimination and inequality erodes a person's sense of worth and belonging. Mental health systems often overlook these realities, resulting in misdiagnosis, inadequate care and further alienation. I witnessed this intimately in Adebayo's life. In the years since his death, I've grappled with how psychotherapy can better support those on the margins. For it to be truly inclusive and healing, it must engage directly with racial trauma, with the violence of homophobia and transphobia, with the vulnerabilities created by Islamophobia and antisemitism, and acknowledge how interlocking systems of oppression impact mental health. This understanding has deepened through client work, workshops, supervision, research and extensive reading around blackness, whiteness and psychoanalytic interventions. I see this book as an extension of that work.

Given that those of us in the health sector will inevitably be helping asylum seekers, refugees and those displaced from war-torn countries, we can be better armed with an understanding of the context in which traumas occurred. This is about truly listening. We can, and must, do better. Just as men are taught not to recognise male privilege, white people are taught not to recognise white privilege. For psychoanalysis to work for all people, we need to make what is invisible, visible. When whiteness views itself as standard or neutral, presuming that what is given to white people is given to Black people too, the result is an erroneous belief that Black people lack something and that they haven't tried hard enough. What white supremacy refuses to acknowledge is that structural and institutional racism keep some within the confines of poverty and marginalisation, while the majority continues to benefit and profit from these unequal systems.

Power and privilege shape every therapeutic encounter. White therapists must remain aware of these systemic imbalances, approaching each client with humility and openness. Awareness without structural understanding remains superficial and performative rather than transformative. True insight requires confronting the realities of power, privilege and the social systems that determine who is seen, heard and healed. If psychoanalysis truly aims to raise awareness, it must acknowledge that most practitioners need better theoretical and practical grounding to understand and support those who live at the margins of society. The work of whiteness involves deep, sustained and often uncomfortable engagement. The work is never finished. The goal isn't mastery but continued openness and accountability.

Psychoanalysis is derived from a European intellectual tradition; the influence of the colonial era remains in reading lists and therapeutic practices. What I am calling for is curiosity. I hope all analysts and therapists can seek influence from outside the traditional Western canon. It's not just what happens in the classroom; it's how we employ what we learn. I am influenced by the independent school – Winnicott, Milner, Bollas, Lacan, Bion, Phillips – who emphasised clinical observation, flexibility, and individual experience over strict adherence to theory. But I am equally influenced by Black feminist writers: Maya Angelou, bell hooks, Audre Lorde, Angela Davies, Patricia Hill-Collins and the work of Franz Fanon and James Baldwin. Thinkers from outside the white canon are too often pushed to the margins of psychoanalytic discourse. Yet there exists a wealth of knowledge rooted in the Black diaspora – in literature, philosophy, psychology, and activism – that offers profound insights into subjectivity, trauma, identity and resistance. We need these voices central to psychoanalytic inquiry, on training reading lists, on library shelves and in homes. These voices are essential to any psychoanalysis that wishes to remain relevant, truthful and inclusive.

One can resonate with a particular school of thinking, but I feel discomfort with training that accentuates specific doctrine. The ability to reproduce Freud, Jung or Klein does not make for a free-thinking or responsive analyst. These theorists were writing from specific historical, cultural and social locations. Their work reflects their time and their biases. A piece of writing, like art or music, exists to generate feelings and thoughts. They exist to inspire us, not to hem us in. A strict, doctrinaire approach won't work for every client, as often their context is vastly different from the context in which the theory emerged, i.e., contemporary, diasporic London versus 19th-century Vienna.

Donald Winnicott's concept of the facilitating environment captures something essential about our role: not to shape or push, but to create conditions in which a person can explore themselves safely and authentically Winnicott, D. W. (1965). This applies far beyond childhood. We become a flexible tool for the client's self-discovery, to be used ethically, always in service of their growth. We should learn alongside them as they learn about themselves.

Central to this is awareness of power dynamics, especially when shaped by race. In many therapeutic spaces, particularly where the therapist is white and the client is Black, there is an added layer of historical and social power imbalance. This dynamic can silence, pathologise or misunderstand the lived experiences of Black clients. What we shouldn't do is hold our own knowledge as absolute truth, reciting what we learned uncritically while contorting a client's story to fit the limits of our doctrine. To do so risks re-enacting the very structures of dominance and erasure that many clients, especially those from racialised or marginalised communities, have spent a lifetime navigating. Instead, we must approach each encounter with openness, curiosity and the humility to know that our understanding is always partial, and that the client's lived truth must take precedence over our theoretical comfort.

My hope is that this book has made the process of therapy more accessible to people thinking of training, considering therapy or currently in therapy. Through psychic change, we can see, hear, speak and listen to one another differently. If we want to change external realities such as social inequality and interpersonal conflict, we must first make the unconscious conscious. This is the foundation of psychic change: a transformation in how we relate to ourselves and others. It requires exploring the unconscious beliefs, fears and identifications we carry, whether tied to power, race, trauma or inherited narratives, and examining how they shape our perceptions, behaviours and relationships. Psychic change is not just intellectual but also emotional and relational. As we become more conscious of what has been hidden or defended against, we open ourselves to seeing, hearing, speaking and listening in new ways – ways that lead to more truthful, compassionate and transformative engagements with the world.

Psychoanalysis is known as the talking cure for good reason. That's why this book has taken the form of dialogue and conversations. A conversation is always two-way. What is reflected often resonates in ways we don't expect. That's the nature of true dialogue–it transforms. For instance, a person experiencing psychosis has much to tell the non-psychotic about life. Psychosis is an extreme state, but an intelligent one, carrying its own logic, its own truths. A psychotic person's narrative suggests that life is confusing, frightening, and that we who are without psychosis may be sleepwalkers in an existence whose true character we are oblivious to. Everyone, regardless of diagnosis or position, has something to teach. If we are willing to listen, even the most disorienting states reveal profound insights: life is complex, meaning is unstable and we are often more asleep to it than we think.

I entered the field with the intention of helping others, but never thought about how psychoanalysis could help me too. Sixteen-plus years later, having been trained in psychoanalytic psychotherapy, I have a deeper understanding of its transformative potential–for myself and for others. Psychotherapy, like life, is a journey rather than a destination. The metaphor I return to is walking down a path; at some point it widens, offering possibilities, curiosity, playfulness and potential; at other times it narrows, becoming more constrained. But even at its most difficult stretches the path holds meaning. It is never static–it's in a constant state of becoming. The training guides us to a point; it gives us tools, language and orientation. But it is at the opening where we take our bearings and continue the journey. That is the essence of psychoanalytic work: a practice of ongoing movement, discovery and becoming.

This pattern emerges in the stories I've told. Many people come with a goal, a point of inertia or presenting problems. They've suffered a breakup, a breakdown or can't get the respect of their colleagues. They feel depressed but aren't sure why. What often emerges is that the presenting problem is a symptom of deeper, underlying issues the individual may not be fully aware of. Through talking, we try to make the unconscious rise to the surface, to give language and shape to what has been hidden and repressed. The client wants a type of life they can visualise but can't seem to obtain. Why? What is standing in their way? What is the resistance? The work is not just about striving towards the imagined life, but about understanding why it remains out of reach. What internal beliefs, fears or identifications are holding the person back? By making the unconscious conscious, the client begins to see not only external obstacles but internal ones, and this recognition allows for true transformation. Transformation begins with this awareness, guided by curiosity, presence and trust.

This book is a testament to the resilience and complexity of Black lives. The stories here – both my own and those of clients – reflect the weight of invisibility, the pressure to perform and the constant negotiation of identity in spaces not designed for our thriving. Yet they also reveal the brilliance, vulnerability and fullness that emerge when one is truly seen; not as a stereotype, but as fully human. Recognition and belonging are not simply granted; they must be claimed. Through therapy, through witnessing, through reflection, we learn to hold ourselves, to name what has been denied, and to reclaim what has been overlooked.

I have a simple wish: to help patients rediscover their desires and their passion for living. At its core, this is about creating conditions in which a person can come to know themselves more fully, not through pressure or prescription, but through presence, safety and trust. We cannot understand others without first understanding ourselves. We cannot change the world without learning to see, listen and hold one another fully.

This book, then, is an invitation: to witness, to listen, to reflect and to create spaces where growth becomes possible. In reading it, I hope you have come to a greater understanding of the need for environments that support this unfolding–the need to make a safe space, a space where growth is facilitated and where people are truly heard. Psychoanalysis, while not the whole story, offers a way of seeing ourselves and each other differently. In that opening, in the practice of bearing witness, lies the possibility for genuine human connection, understanding and transformation.

To be seen is not merely to exist–it is to matter.

Acknowledgements

I am grateful to so many who have supported me in writing this book.

Adam Phillips, your unwavering presence and the many conversations we have shared over the years have been a profound force in my life. I am deeply grateful.

Danai Denga, you brought such care and attention to this material. Your thoughtful engagement meant a great deal.

Adebayo, my brother, your love and boundless optimism about life have been a light throughout this journey, and you remain a light.

To my family, thank you for believing in me through every stage of this process. Your faith in me has been a foundation I have leaned on more than you know.

DA, thank you for reading this work with such care, for the thoughtful edits, and for your encouragement at the moments I needed it most.

Bibliography

1. Alleyne, A. (2004). Black identity and workplace oppression. Counselling and Psychotherapy Research, 4(1), 4–8.
2. Bhui, K., Halvorsrud, K., & Nazroo, J. (2018). Making a difference: ethnic inequality and severe mental illness.
3. *British Journal of Psychiatry, 213*(4), 574–578. https://doi.org/10.1192/bjp.2018.148
4. Black Talent Charter in collaboration with Bain & Company. (2024). *Why we need to pick up the pace of Black representation in finance and professional services in the UK*. Black Talent Charter. https://www.bain.com/insights/why-we-need-to-pick-up-the-pace-of-black-representation-in-finance-and-professional-services-in-the-uk-report/
5. Bollas, C. (1992). Being a character: Psychoanalysis and self-experience. London: Routledge.

6. British Association for Counselling and Psychotherapy (BACP). (2023). Facts and figures about counselling and psychotherapy. Retrieved from https://www.bacp.co.uk
7. Clark, K. B., & Clark, M. P. (1947). Racial identification and preference in Negro children. Journal of Negro Education, 16(3), 341–350.
8. Crenshaw, K. (1991). Mapping the margins: Intersectionality, identity politics, and violence against women of color. *Stanford Law Review, 43*(6), 1241–1299.
9. Dalal, F. (2002). Race, colour and the processes of racialization: new perspectives from group analysis, psychoanalysis and sociology. Hove: Brunner-Routledge.
10. Davies, J. (2021). Sedated: How modern capitalism created our mental health crisis. London: Atlantic Books.
11. DiAngelo, R. (2018). *White fragility: Why it's so hard for white people to talk about racism.* Boston: Beacon Press
12. Fanon, F. (1967). Black skin, white masks (C. L. Markmann, Trans.). New York: Grove Press. (Original work published 1952)
13. Foucault, M. (1965). Madness and civilization: A history of insanity in the age of reason (R. Howard, Trans.). New York: Pantheon Books.
14. Gov.UK. (16 August 2024). Detentions under the Mental Health Act. Ethnicity facts and figures. Retrieved from https://www.ethnicity-facts-figures.service.gov.uk/health/mental-health/detentions-under-the-mental-health-act/latest

15. Grier, W. H., & Cobbs, P. M. (1968). Black rage. New York: Basic Books.
16. Hardy, K. V., & Laszloffy, T. A. (2005). Teens who hurt: Clinical interventions to break the cycle of adolescent violence. New York: Guilford Press.
17. Holmes, D. E. (1992). Race and transference in psychoanalysis and psychotherapy. International Journal of Psychoanalysis, 73(1), 1–11.
18. Holmes, D. E. (2016). Culturally imposed trauma: The sleeping dog has awakened. Will psychoanalysis take heed? Psychoanalytic Dialogues, 26(6), 641–654.
19. hooks, b. (1981). Ain't I a Woman: Black Women and Sexism. South End Press.
20. hooks, b. (2000). Where we stand: Class matters. New York: Routledge.
21. House of Commons Women and Equalities Committee. (2023). Black Maternal Health. House of Commons.
22. Kleinman, A. (1988). The illness narratives: Suffering, healing, and the human condition. New York: Basic Books.
23. Laing, R. D. (1967). The politics of experience. New York: Pantheon Books.
24. Menakem, R. (2017). My grandmother's hands: Racialized trauma and the pathway to mending our hearts and bodies. Las Vegas: Central Recovery Press.
25. Norcross, J. C., & Lambert, M. J. (2018). Psychotherapy relationships that work III. Psychotherapy, 55(4), 303–315.

26. Office for National Statistics. (2023). Ethnicity pay gaps in Great Britain: 2012 to 2022. ONS. https://www.ons.gov.uk/employmentandlabourmarket/peopleinwork/earningsandworkinghours/articles/ethnicitypaygapsingreatbritain/2012to2022
27. Orange, D. M. (2011). The suffering stranger: Hermeneutics for everyday clinical practice. New York: Routledge.
28. Ryde, J. (2009). Being white in the helping professions: Developing effective intercultural awareness. London: Jessica Kingsley Publishers
29. Sardar, Z. (2008). Foreword. In F. Fanon, Black skin, white masks (pp. vii–xliii). Pluto Press.Stern, D. N. (2004). The present moment in psychotherapy and everyday life. New York: W. W. Norton.
30. Szasz, T. S. (1961). The myth of mental illness: Foundations of a theory of personal conduct. New York: Harper & Row.
31. Wampold, B. E. (2015). How important are the common factors in psychotherapy? An update. World Psychiatry, 14(3), 270–277.
32. Winicott, D. W. (1971). Playing and reality. London: Tavistock Publications.

About the Author

Abi Canepa-Anson is a psychodynamic psychotherapist, writer and activist with more than 16 years of clinical experience. She is the author of *Parenting The Adopted Child: Beyond Love and Intention*.

Committed to demystifying therapy and making it genuinely accessible–particularly to those marginalised by race, culture and systemic inequality–her work bridges psychological insight with lived experience across individual, couple and group settings, and extends into clinical supervision. She has worked in a psychiatric hospital, with a disordered eating unit and in higher education, and leads workshops and teaches on postgraduate courses for Equity, Diversity and Inclusion.

Trained at WPF (Westminster Pastoral Foundation), the British Psychotherapy Foundation, with additional training in relationship and psychosexual therapy and group supervision, Abi explores psychotherapy through an intersectional lens, holding race, faith, culture and inherited identity together as inseparable threads, and illuminating both the transformative potential of that work and its limits. She has been in conversation with some of the field's leading thinkers, including Adam Phillips, on the traumas of racism and the limits of psychoanalysis. Her writing and work examine adoption, diasporic histories and questions of identity, belonging and systemic inequality.

Alongside her clinical and literary work, Abi is a mixed-media artist.

Connect with the Author

To learn more about the author's work or upcoming projects, visit:

www.abicatherapy.com

www.youtube.com/@abicanepa-anson

www.ingramcontent.com/pod-product-compliance
Lightning Source LLC
LaVergne TN
LVHW050101160926
848065LV00029B/229
9781918992083